I0050581

Outlook improving, but challenges and uncertainty remain

A stronger economic recovery is underway on the back of vaccination progress, better-calibrated public health measures, and extraordinary fiscal and monetary policy support. The global economy is forecast to grow by 6.0% in 2021 and 4.4% in 2022, with developing Asia growing by 7.2% (2021) and 5.4% (2022). The latest numbers represent an improved, though still highly uncertain, outlook over the previous forecast. Meanwhile, economic prospects between countries and across sectors are diverging. Much will depend on the race between the virus spread—including new variants—and vaccination rate; sustained fiscal stimulus and international coordination to limit economic scarring; and the evolution of monetary policy settings in tandem with financial conditions and inflation risks. The direction and interaction of these factors will determine whether the balance of risks will tilt to the upside or downside.

After a coronavirus disease (COVID-19) pandemic-induced economic contraction of 5.8% in 2020, the Pacific is expected to recover with moderate growth of 0.3% in 2021 and 4.0% in 2022. The outlook reflects growth prospects for Papua New Guinea, the subregion's largest economy, where a modest recovery is projected this year before strengthening next year. Travel bubbles are expected to contribute to gradual recovery in some smaller Pacific economies, such as the Cook Islands and Niue, because of their economic ties with New Zealand. Highlighting the risks of travel bubbles, however, the arrangement between Palau and Taipei,China earlier this year collapsed after a surge in cases in the latter. Instead, Palau has opened its borders to fully vaccinated travelers, as long as they can travel or transit through Guam (where the remaining twice-weekly flight originates). Similarly, widespread vaccination, both within Pacific economies and in their major economic partners, is expected to play a major role in boosting growth in 2022.

Growth in the United States (US) economy is forecast to accelerate substantially to 6.5% in 2021 before moderating to 4.4% in 2022. Gross domestic product (GDP) is expected to have returned to pre–COVID-19 pandemic levels by the second quarter of this year because of increasing vaccination coverage and sizeable fiscal support. The government's rescue package, along with continued accommodative monetary policy, pose positive spillovers for US major trading partners and the global economy at large. Risks to the outlook, however, are tilted to the downside, and depend largely on the effectiveness of the vaccination effort.

The People's Republic of China (PRC) will continue to lead East Asia's recovery in 2021 on the back of rising private consumption and strong exports. GDP growth is forecast at 8.1% this year from a low base, and 5.5% growth in 2022. In the first quarter (Q1) of 2021, the PRC economy expanded by 18.3% year-on-year (y-o-y) on strong expansion in industrial production, retail sales, investment, and exports. GDP growth is expected to gradually moderate in the succeeding quarters this year and into 2022. Downside risks include the sporadic emergence of new COVID-19 clusters, uncertainty on whether growth in household demand can be sustained, persistent finance sector risks, and a deterioration in external trade and technology access.

The Japanese economy struggled in Q1 2021, with preliminary estimates of an annualized 5.1% decline as a third wave of COVID-19 cases emerged in January. Private investment fell by 5.5% and public spending by 6.9%. The latest waves of COVID-19 cases have delayed economic recovery, but the economy is seen to bounce back in the second half of 2021 and through 2022 as the vaccination rollout accelerates. Nevertheless, the possibility of renewed surges in cases, the speed of vaccination, and the possibility of increased transmission at the Tokyo Olympics remain as downside risks. GDP is forecast to grow by 2.6% this year and 2.7% in 2022.

Australia's economy expanded in the first quarter of 2021, supported by private sector investment and household spending. Seasonally adjusted GDP

GDP Growth (%, annual)

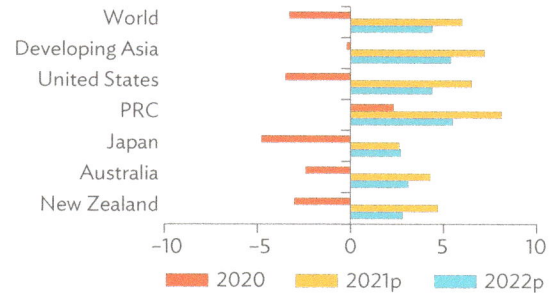

DMC = developing member country, GDP = gross domestic product, p = projection, PRC = People's Republic of China.
Notes: Developing Asia and Pacific DMCs as defined by ADB. Figures are based on ADB estimates except for world GDP growth.
Sources: ADB. 2021. *Asian Development Outlook 2021: Financing a Green and Inclusive Recovery.* Manila; ADB. 2021. *Asian Development Outlook Supplement July 2021.* Manila; International Monetary Fund. 2021. *World Economic Outlook April 2021: Managing Divergent Recoveries.* Washington, DC.

GDP Growth in Developing Asia (%, annual)

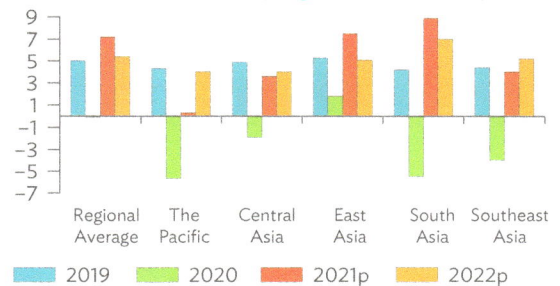

GDP = gross domestic product, p = projection.
Source: ADB. 2021. *Asian Development Outlook Supplement July 2021.* Manila.

COVID-19 Cases in Pacific Developing Member Countries

	Total cases	Active cases	Total deaths	Total cases /1,000 population
Papua New Guinea	17,340	186	179	1.76
Fiji	12,666	10,062	69	13.99
Solomon Islands	20	–	–	0.03
Marshall Islands	4	–	–	0.07
Vanuatu	4	–	1	0.01
Samoa	3	–	–	0.01
FSM	1	–	–	0.01
World	189,190,520	12,300,516	4,074,788	23.95

FSM = Federated States of Micronesia.
Note: Data as of 15 July 2021.
Sources: ADB. Asian Development Outlook Datasheet (accessed 30 June 2021); Worldometer. Worldometer COVID-19 Data and Population (accessed 15 July 2021).

Average Spot Price of Brent Crude Oil
(monthly, $/barrel)

Source: World Bank Commodity Price Data (Pink Sheet).

Export Prices of Selected Commodities
(2018 = 100, annual)

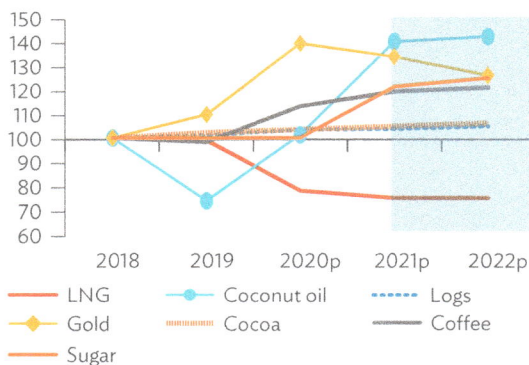

LNG = liquefied natural gas, p = projection.
Source: Asian Development Bank calculations using data from World Bank Commodity Price Data (Pink Sheets).

Tourist Departures to Pacific Destinations
('000 persons, January–April totals)

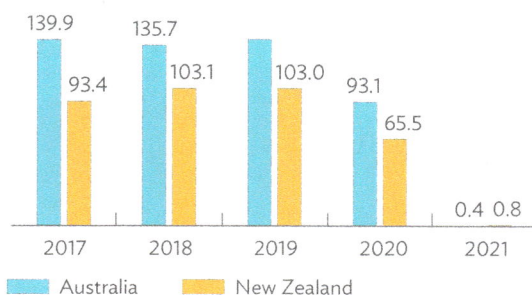

Note: Pacific destinations include the Cook Islands, Fiji, Samoa, Tonga, and Vanuatu.
Sources: Australian Bureau of Statistics and Statistics New Zealand.

Lead authors: Remrick Patagan, Noel Del Castillo, and Rommel Rabanal

rose by 1.8% in Q1, reflecting success in containing COVID-19 combined wit a fiscal and monetary stimulus. Consensus Forecasts projects the economy t grow by 4.3% in 2021 and 3.1% in 2022. The speed of the vaccine rollout an duration of its border closure will significantly affect the outlook.

- In New Zealand, housing booms and strong retail spending drove economi recovery in the first quarter of 2021 as GDP grew by 1.6%. Aside from a surgin housing sector, households recorded higher spending on accommodatio eating out, appliances, and motor vehicles. Businesses invested in plants an machinery, and transport equipment. Consensus Forecasts expects the Ne Zealand economy to grow by 4.7% in 2021 and 2.8% in 2022. While the viru has been virtually eliminated in the country, a sluggish vaccine rollout an continued border closure cloud this outlook.

Commodity price prospects remain uncertain amid the threat of new pandemic wave

- Brent crude oil prices have steadily risen in the past several months, posting 20.0% y-o-y increase in the first quarter of 2021. Crude oil prices are expected t rise by 33.6% in 2021 as oil demand strengthens, buoyed by vaccination rollout and economic recovery momentum. However, new waves of COVID-19 an consequent restrictions that adversely affect demand, particularly for transpor pose a downside risk. Prices of agricultural commodities continue to rise wit the global food price index jumping by 25.8% in the first quarter of 2021, drive by production shortfalls. The index is forecast to increase by 15.2% for 2021 as whole with a modest reduction in 2022.

- Prices of liquefied natural gas fell by 4.0% in the first quarter of 2021, drive by weakened demand because of the global economic recession and recen abundant supply. The full-year 2021 price forecast is for a 4.8% drop, and th downward trend is expected to continue in succeeding years. Cocoa price have been broadly stable and are expected to remain so over the forecas period. On the other hand, the average price of Arabica coffee went up b 16.0% in the first quarter of 2021. A sharp reduction in global supply, becaus of a projected decline in Brazil's coffee production, will sustain the Arabic price gain in the early part of this year. Although gold prices were up by 13.6% in the first quarter of 2021, they are expected to fall over the remainder of the year as production rebounds from the COVID-19 restrictions.

Travel bubbles offer temporary relief to Pacific tourism

- Tourism to the Pacific remains largely closed, with arrivals during January–April 202 plunging by 99%–100% y-o-y. Some Pacific destinations are looking to safe trave bubbles to provide relief to ailing tourism sectors. Palau implemented a quarantine-free travel bubble with Taipei,China—its third largest source of tourists—in Apri with twice-weekly flights each carrying up to 100 passengers. However, high cost and strict health protocols limited the number of inbound tourists to under 30C and the bubble was suspended after 7 weeks because of rising COVID-19 cases ir Taipei,China. Palau's experience highlights the delicate balance between health and economic concerns that threaten the sustainability of such arrangements.

- Australia and New Zealand have been successful in containing COVID-19, allowing for the start of a quarantine-free trans-Tasman travel bubble between the two countries in April 2021. Although recent outbreaks in Victoria (in May) and New South Wales (in June) have led to a partial suspension of these arrangements expansion of the trans-Tasman bubble to safely include Pacific countries is possible later this year. New Zealand already has arrangements with the Cook Islands and Niue. Quarantine-free travel from the Cook Islands to New Zealand has operated intermittently since January 2021 and, in May, the Cook Islands likewise allowed quarantine-free flights from New Zealand. The number of visitors has exceeded expectations, with Cook Islands tourism officials now projecting visitor arrivals to reach 50%–60% of pre-pandemic numbers in the coming months, provided both parties remain free of COVID-19. Quarantine-free flights from New Zealand to Niue commenced in March, with ongoing discussions on reciprocal travel after the completion of vaccination rollout in Niue. Australia has had initial discussions on similar bubble arrangements with Solomon Islands, Tonga, and Vanuatu, but dialogue with Fiji has been deferred likely until the ongoing outbreak in Fiji is contained.

"Travel bubbles of hope" in the Cook Islands, Niue, and Palau

Lead authors: Lily Anne Homasi, Rommel Rabanal, and James Webb

The Cook Islands, Niue, and Palau share many similarities with relatively small populations that have enjoyed considerable improvements in living standards over the past two decades, largely because of their attractiveness as tourist destinations. All three economies have been severely affected by restrictions on international travel related to the coronavirus disease (COVID-19), and their priority is to reopen to tourists as a matter of urgency to support economic recovery. Further, all three have strong ties to a major trade and development partners, including pathways for migration. Each has pursued travel bubbles with a major tourism market alongside an aggressive vaccination program, with the assistance of their major bilateral development partners in the sourcing and distribution of vaccines (New Zealand for the Cook Islands and Niue, and the United States [US] for Palau). This article explores the similarities and differences in their respective approaches, the risks, and the recent performance.

PALAU

With sustained progress since the start of its national vaccination program as early as January 2021, Palau has now fully vaccinated more than 95% of its adult population against COVID-19. This is well above the vaccination rates recorded not only among its North Pacific peers but globally as well. In turn, high vaccination uptake has allowed Palau to consider and implement interim steps toward full reopening of its tourism-dependent economy, which is seen to contract by a cumulative 18% during fiscal year (FY) 2020 (that ended on 30 September 2020) and FY2021, resulting in substantial adverse impacts on households and businesses.

On 1 April 2021, Palau commenced a safe travel bubble with Taipei,China. Pre-pandemic, Taipei,China was among Palau's top three sources of tourists, with annual arrivals averaging about 13,000 or about 11% of total arrivals during FY2015–FY2019. Under the travel bubble arrangement, two weekly roundtrip flights brought tourists from Taipei,China to Palau on Wednesdays and Saturdays. These were the first commercial flights allowed to bring international tourists into Palau since borders closed in March 2020. The maximum number of passengers was 110 per flight, which translates to 880 per month or 2,640 per quarter compared with annual arrivals of almost 90,000 in FY2019 (14,000 of which were from Taipei,China). However, only the first few flights were fully booked, with those thereafter at under 50% capacity.

Key considerations for tourists included high costs and stringent health protocols to guard against community exposure. A 4-day tour package cost about $2,400–$3,000, more than double the pre-pandemic cost of about $1,000. Also, strict health surveillance and infection prevention and control measures applied to tour participants included (i) undergoing a polymerase chain reaction (PCR) test at the airport before boarding, which means travelers need to be at the airport more than 5 hours before the flight; (ii) proof of no international travel within the past 6 months, no record of COVID-19 infection within the past 3 months, and no quarantine within the past 2 months; (iii) staying within tour groups, keeping away from locals, and only using pre-arranged transport, accommodation, restaurants, and other establishments while in Palau; and (iv) "enhanced" monitoring upon return, with a follow-up PCR test at a hospital 5 days after arrival in Taipei,China.

Both parties were hopeful that uptake of bubble flights would increase during Taipei,China's summer months of June–September, with some judicious adjustments to health protocols. Unfortunately, the bubble burst in mid-May 2021 amid rising COVID-19 cases in Taipei,China. Over its 7 weeks in operation, the safe travel bubble brought fewer than 300 tourists into Palau—which is only about 2% of total pre-pandemic arrivals during the months of April and May—but nonetheless provided valuable firsthand experience in partially reopening borders while keeping health risks contained.

Toward the end of May 2021, Palau further opened its borders to fully vaccinated people from the US and its territories via twice-monthly flights from Guam. Such travelers still need approval from the Palau Quarantine Office, which requires a negative PCR test within 72 hours of departure date from Guam, but they will no longer be required to stay at a quarantine hotel. Instead, they will be subjected to restricted movement for 7 days, after which another PCR test is conducted on-island. This process had effectively contained infection risks, with Palau's only two COVID-19 positive tests on record both confirmed to be historical cases from infections contracted by travelers well before travelling to the country. On 4 July 2021, Palau further eased restrictions, now only requiring travelers to present airline representatives with proof of full vaccination—with the final dose received at least 14 days prior to arrival—and a negative PCR test result taken no more than 3 days prior to departure.

To further prepare for broader reopening and more sustainable recovery from the COVID-19 crisis, the government continues to provide temporary assistance to the private sector through its Coronavirus Relief One-Stop Shop Program that comprises unemployment benefits, temporary employment schemes, expanded lifeline utility subsidies, and interest-free lending to businesses. The government is also embarking on a wide-ranging reform agenda to (i) strengthen the policy and legislative framework for public financial management; (ii) reduce fiscal risks from weak management of public revenue (e.g., tax reform), expenditure (e.g., infrastructure investment planning), and liabilities (e.g., social security reform); and (iii) support further private sector development to shift Palau's economic recovery from the COVID-19 crisis toward a more sustainable fiscal path. Taken together, these measures may help facilitate a stronger and swifter rebound in the near-term, provided that steady progress in reopening the economy and restarting tourism is also achieved.

COOK ISLANDS

The Cook Islands has been one of the hardest hit economies in the Pacific because of the COVID-19 pandemic. Although there have been no local COVID-19 cases since the start of the pandemic, the country faces unprecedented economic challenges from the collapse in tourism.

Border closures delayed construction activities and eliminated tourist arrivals from April 2020 to early May 2021. The Cook Islands economy contracted by 5.2% in FY2020 (ended 30 June 2020) compared to growth of 5.3% in FY2019. The government, through its Economic Response Plan, has mitigated the impact of the contraction on the economy and livelihoods. Economic activity is estimated to have contracted by a further 26.0% in FY2021. A gradual recovery is expected to gain momentum following the commencement of the quarantine-free travel bubble between the Cook Islands and New Zealand on 17 May 2021. For May and June, the Cook Islands recorded 1,486 and 6,054 visitors, respectively.[1] This is about 10.3% of May arrivals and 37.9% of June arrivals in 2019. The government expects flights per week to increase from 6 to 11 on 16 August, carrying more than 200 visitors per flight, and about 12 or more weekly flights in November onwards. Visitors from New Zealand alone (the main tourist market for the Cook Islands) averaged 66.8% of total visitor arrivals between FY2016 and FY2019 (Figure 1).

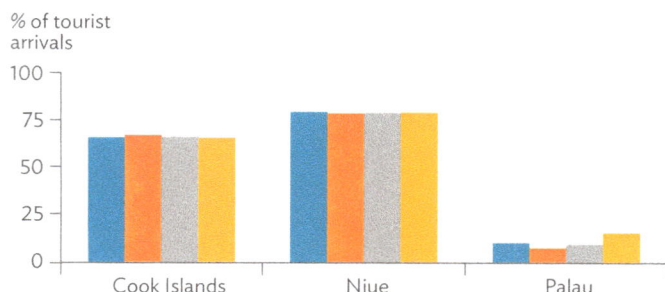

Figure 1: Share of Travel Bubble Partner in Total Visitor Arrivals

FY = fiscal year.
Note: Travel bubble partner refers to New Zealand for the Cook Islands and Niue, and the United States for Palau.
Sources: Governments of the Cook Islands, Niue, and Palau.

Prior to the commencement of the travel bubble, the government embarked on a comprehensive set of initiatives to support its readiness to receive visitors. These included establishing a COVID-19 website[2] to clearly communicate COVID-19-related updates, launching a contact tracing mobile application, training frontline health and immigration staff on enforcing COVID-19 measures (and administering the COVID-19 vaccine, in the case of selected health workers), and establishing a PCR laboratory. These and other related activities were overseen by the Border Easement Task Force (comprising the Prime Minister and senior government officials from the ministries of foreign affairs and immigration, health, and finance and economic management) to expedite the operationalization of two-way quarantine-free travel. These initiatives not only gained the confidence of New Zealand authorities to open its borders to the Cook Islands but provided the Cook Islands with tools to test, track, trace, and ensure the safety of Cook Islanders and visitors to the country. Negotiations at the political level between governments helped a great deal to formally establish the bubble with New Zealand.

To further strengthen the Cook Islands' readiness to receive visitors, the government, through the support of the Government of New Zealand (its main bilateral development partner), rolled out COVID-19 vaccines from May 2021 for the 10,189 eligible population. As of 23 June 2021, the Ministry of Health of the Cook Islands reported that 95.7% and 90.2% of the eligible population have received the first and second doses, respectively.[3] Those on the more remote islands are expected to be fully vaccinated by the third quarter of 2021. With these initial positive signs, the economy is expected to recover in FY2022 as the continuation of quarantine-free travel promotes economic activity.

Downside risks remain, however: should there be local transmission of COVID-19 in New Zealand or the Cook Islands both governments have shown that they may unilaterally close the travel arrangements, which would halt the travel bubble and further deteriorate the Cook Islands' already battered economic and fiscal position.

NIUE

Through preemptive action to prevent the entry of COVID-19, Niue has successfully safeguarded its capacity-constrained health system from the potentially catastrophic impacts of the disease on its vulnerable population. Borders have been effectively closed since March 2020, with only a limited number of passenger flights allowed entry to bring in returning residents and essential workers. Tourists from New Zealand—which accounted for about 80% of arrivals prior to the pandemic—plunged to a total of only 61 during April–December 2020 from more than 6,000 during the same period of the preceding year. This has continued in 2021, with only 33 arrivals in January–April.

Pre-pandemic tourism receipts amounted to about a third of annual gross domestic product. The pause in international tourism has severely impacted business activity in Niue, as a significant share of businesses depends heavily on demand from tourists. Based on a series of surveys by Pacific Trade Invest Australia, about 37% of businesses in Niue were either temporarily or permanently closed as of May 2021 (Figure 2). This is below the peak of 42% recorded in February, but still above the average for the survey period covering June 2020–May 2021. Further, about 32% are not confident that their business can survive the ongoing COVID-19 crisis. These trends highlight the potential "scarring" or loss in long-term supply capacity that can result from a severe and prolonged downturn.

The arrival of COVID-19 vaccines in June was a critical milestone that has opened a clear path toward safely reopening and revitalizing the tourism-based economy. Niue's small population of only about 1,700

ends itself to a swift rollout that can achieve herd immunity relatively quickly. With assistance from New Zealand, Niue vaccinated 97% of the population aged 16 and above over a period of about 5 weeks ending in early July, thereby achieving herd immunity.

Figure 2: Status and Sentiments of Businesses in Niue

% of businesses surveyed

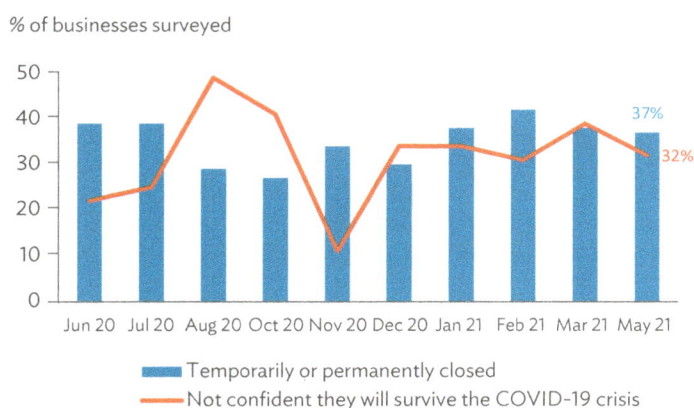

COVID-19 = coronavirus disease.
Source: Pacific Trade Invest Pacific Business Monitor (various issues).

In turn, completion of the vaccination program will allow for gradual reopening of Niue's borders to international travelers. This will likely begin with the implementation of a full quarantine-free travel bubble with New Zealand, reciprocating current arrangements that have permitted one-way travel from Niue to New Zealand since March 2021. Further reopening to other neighbors in the Pacific and Oceania can follow, subject to vaccination progress in partner countries.

Gradual but safe reopening will be the key to restarting Niue's tourism sector and reviving business activity. These can then help underpin sustainable economic recovery and regain lost progress and momentum toward achieving desired longer-term development outcomes.

LESSONS FOR THE PACIFIC SUBREGION

The Cook Islands, Niue, and Palau represent the most likely countries to have successful quarantine-free travel with at least one of their major tourism markets over the coming 6 months, but what lessons can be drawn for the broader Pacific subregion?

First, vaccination rates for the Cook Islands, Niue, and Palau are extremely high, even by global standards. These countries have low vaccine hesitancy and have relied almost exclusively on a larger partner government to source and assist in administering the vaccinations. This includes concurrent capacity-building programs for country officials, cold-chain management, and the mobilization of specialist teams to assist in the rollout. In the case of the Cook Islands, the vaccination challenge equates to less than 1 day's worth of vaccinations for a country the size of New Zealand—the

comparison for the US and Palau, or New Zealand and Niue, is even more dramatic. This means that the capacity diversion and vaccine supply for the partner government from their own vaccination efforts is miniscule compared to their own domestic vaccination challenges.

This links to the second common element: all three economies are small, both in terms of population and logistical hurdles. Outside of the resource diversion that vaccinating a larger Pacific country like Fiji or Papua New Guinea presents, the vast majority of the populations of each country live on the main island: for Palau, 64.8% of the population live in the capital, Koror, with another 29.4% on the adjoining island of Babeldaob; in the Cook Islands 74.6% live on Rarotonga; and Niue is only one island. In terms of logistics, the presence of an international airport, health facilities, and government offices on these hubs greatly smooths the first stage of any vaccination rollout. Beyond the main islands, inter-island logistics are also relatively easy by Pacific standards: in Palau, all states except Hatohobei and Sonsorol can be reached by boat within half a day; and while the Cook Islands covers 2 million square kilometers of ocean, almost all the inhabited islands except for Nassau, Palmerston, and Rakahanga (all with less than 100 people) have a functioning airstrip that can land enough supplies to vaccinate the whole island. The vaccine types used also facilitated shorter periods between doses, enabling the repeat visits to remote locations to be tightly scheduled.

Third, all three countries were free of COVID-19 prior to both their vaccination drives and their attempts to open travel bubbles. Indeed, this was the case for most of the Pacific island countries, with Fiji and Papua New Guinea being perhaps the only countries outside of the US and French territories to have significant outbreaks of COVID-19 in the past 12 months. This bodes well for other nations who have managed to keep COVID-19 at bay, but will not be encouraging for Fiji, which may have to rely on vaccinations as the only pathway for an economic recovery (a discussion on the experience in Fiji is on pp. 9–11).

Fourth, large sections of the private sector in all three countries would face bankruptcy if tourism does not return. Fiscal support programs have been enacted across the board, but these cannot continue indefinitely, with fiscal resources coming under increasing pressure. With the absence of central banks in all three countries to support the economy as lender of last resort, this fiscal pressure could potentially lead to fiscal liquidity issues, exacerbating an already dire situation (Figure 3).

This creates a strong incentive for policymakers, government officials, development partners, and the private sector to work closely together on reopening borders, including successful rollouts of vaccination programs. It is not just a question of health, but also of economic survival, and this may at least partially explain the low vaccine hesitancy rates thus far. Importantly, an economic collapse would likely trigger mass migration in search of employment opportunities, as all three countries have preferential access to the labor markets of their largest trading partners (US and New Zealand).

Figure 3: Fiscal Balance of the Cook Islands, Niue, and Palau

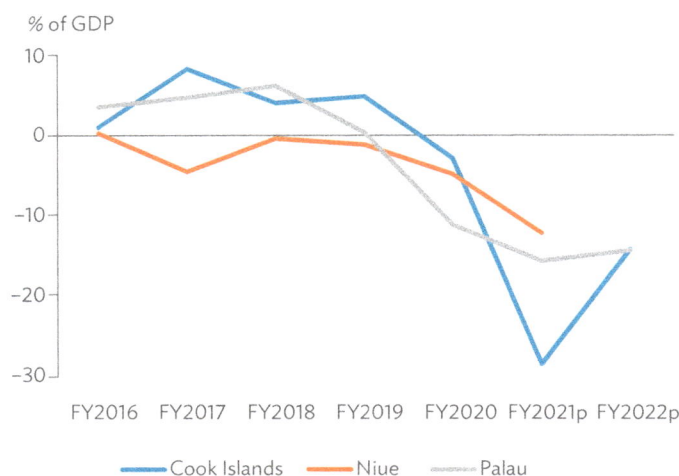

% of GDP

FY = fiscal year, GDP = gross domestic product, p = projection.
Note: Fiscal year ends 30 June for the Cook Islands and Niue, and 30 September for Palau.
Sources: Asian Development Outlook and Pacific Economic Monitor databases.

Last, the travel bubbles are with major tourism source markets that had either contained the virus (New Zealand) or effectively controlled widespread outbreaks (Taipei,China). This is where the risk profile of the tourist-source market is an important factor. Globally, New Zealand stands out as an "elimination country" that has had few community cases of COVID-19 and gone for extended periods with no such cases at all. This means that vaccination is preferred, but not essential, in both the tourist-source and tourism-destination markets. On the other hand, Taipei,China has shown success pursuing a "suppression" strategy that until the recent outbreak was successful at lowering, but not eliminating, the risk to the tourist-destination market and required at least the frontline and tourism-facing workers to be vaccinated and separate from the unvaccinated population. With more countries increasing the coverage of vaccinations, a third type of source market for vaccinated travelers may also be possible; and indeed Palau has already partially opened this option for US travelers, with some mitigation efforts to control for breakthrough infections.

Combined, these elements suggest that, if countries can address vaccine hesitancy, smaller Pacific nations have ready examples in terms of an effective rollout strategy and reopening. Particularly Samoa and Tonga may be able to tap into the Cook Islands' experience to join a pan-Pacific "Oceania" or "Pacific bubble," as they have many of the shared characteristics that have made the Cook Islands strategy effective thus far, including a close relationship with their likely tourism-source markets of New Zealand and Australia. The first steps have already commenced with seasonal workers from these countries, and this could provide an expanding pathway towards reopening as vaccination rates continue to improve. The

main islands in Samoa (Upolu) and Tonga (Tongatapu) also host the vast majority of the national populations, although delivering the vaccine to the outer islands in Tonga may prove more challenging.

Beyond Polynesia, the picture is less clear, as recent outbreaks in Fiji and Australia have removed the "COVID-19-free" precursors that existed in the New Zealand and the Cook Islands examples. For these countries, vaccination will play a much larger role in the immediate term.

In the Central Pacific, logistical challenges, limited capacity, and vaccine hesitancy in some groups in Kiribati and Tuvalu will complicate vaccine rollout. Similar challenges are also evident in the Federated States of Micronesia and the Marshall Islands, where despite early access to vaccines through the US, rollout is being slowed by geographic dispersion of the population (see pp. 16–17). Conversely, Nauru's single island geography has allowed for a rapid vaccination rollout (p. 19), as also seen in Niue.

In conclusion, the Cook Islands, Niue, and Palau are leading the subregion on these "travel bubbles." Factors such as leadership, timely implementation of activities to boost readiness, and timely rollout of vaccination have been critical. However, risks of community transmission in the parties to the bubble remain, even with partial vaccination. Such risks may disrupt efforts and economic recovery in the Cook Islands and Niue, as it has done in Palau. Vaccination remains the surest way of ensuring a sustainable recovery in both the short and long term, but there are other options for those that have kept COVID-19 at bay.

Endnotes

[1] Government of the Cook Islands, Ministry of Finance and Economic Management.

[2] https://covid19.gov.ck/.

[3] As at 23 June 2021, 9,755 first doses and 9,187 second doses had been administered to a total eligible population of 10,189 (Cook Islands Ministry Health).

References

ADB. 2021. *Asian Development Outlook 2021: Financing a Green and Inclusive Recovery.* Manila.

Government of the Cook Islands. 2016. *Cook Islands Population Census 2016.* Rarotonga.

Government of the Cook Islands. *COVID-19 Cook Islands Response.* https://www.health.gov.ck/covid19/vaccination (accessed 5 July 2021).

Treading a fine line: assessing Fiji's economic recovery efforts amid a new pandemic wave

Lead author: Isoa Wainiqolo

On 19 March 2020, Fiji recorded its first case of the coronavirus disease (COVID-19). International borders were closed, and "hard" lockdowns were imposed to minimize transmission. The country successfully contained the virus with no community transmission for almost a full year. On 18 April 2021, a protocol breach at a quarantine facility started the second wave. The first community carrier later attended a funeral gathering, which health authorities labelled as the super-spreader event that triggered the current outbreak. Genomic sequencing later confirmed the highly contagious Delta coronavirus variant was involved.

PRE-PANDEMIC ECONOMY AND PUBLIC HEALTH

Fiji enjoyed an unprecedented 9 years of consecutive growth from 2010 up to 2018. Growth was supported by public and private investments. The former was supported by robust government revenues and the latter by a low interest environment. Tourism and travel related services remained the main contributors to the growth during this period and, to a much lesser extent, the agriculture sector. Tourism and related services are estimated to have contributed 34% to gross domestic product (GDP) and 26% to total employment. The central bank estimates that tourism and related services provided about a third of total government revenue in 2019.[1]

The domestic economy plateaued in 2019 as the government started to rein in fiscal support while the global economy also slowed. Government debt had been on a downward trajectory from 2010 to 2015, falling from 56.2% of GDP to 43%, partly because there were relatively few severe tropical cyclones in this period that necessitated borrowing for major rehabilitation expenditures. Debt increased thereafter, reaching 49.3% of GDP in 2019, after the government had to spend F$500 million over a 3-year period (2016–2019) to finance rehabilitation efforts following severe tropical cyclones Winston (February 2016), Josie and Keni (both in April 2018).

In terms of the health sector, noncommunicable diseases (NCDs), such as high blood pressure, heart and lung problems, diabetes, obesity, and cancer, contributed to 44% of deaths among persons aged 15–34 in the 2012–2017 period and this proportion increased to 75% among adults aged 35–59.[2] About 10% of the populace is aged 60 years and above based on the 2017 census. Old age and medical conditions related to pre-existing NCDs have been identified as high-risk factors for COVID-19 according to the World Health Organization (WHO). In addition, most Fijians do not undergo frequent medical checkups unless required for employment or migration purposes. Instead, many patients visit hospitals when it is already too late for medical care. The coverage of voluntary health insurance is limited in Fiji, mainly through employer-based schemes or employee-based union membership.

The number of fatalities is now rising, and the high prevalence of NCDs before the pandemic means that more lives are likely to be lost if the current outbreak deteriorates further. Fiji's young population with a median age of 27.5 years, lower than the median age of 30.3 years in Asia and 32.6 years in Oceania, provides some mitigation, but recent statistics suggest more Fijians are dying young because of NCDs, and comorbidities put them at risk of COVID-19 too.

LOCAL OUTBREAK IN 2021

Three months into the 2021 outbreak, as of 18 July, the number of cases has grown to 17,444 in the current outbreak with 96 fatalities plus 41 COVID-19-positive patients assessed as having died because of pre-existing conditions.[3] It is unclear when the outbreak will peak, with the highest daily number of confirmed cases so far, 1,405, recorded on 16 July. Measured per million people on a 7-day moving average basis, the current number of confirmed cases exceeds past peaks in the Pacific subregion[4] and in Brazil, India, the United Kingdom, and the United States (Figure 4). On 30 June 2021, Fiji had the fastest doubling time of confirmed cases among all countries. On the same day, the Ministry of Health announced a new strategy where isolation facilities will be dedicated to patients who are most at risk of becoming ill or dying from the virus. Other patients will be asked to self-isolate and undergo home-based care.

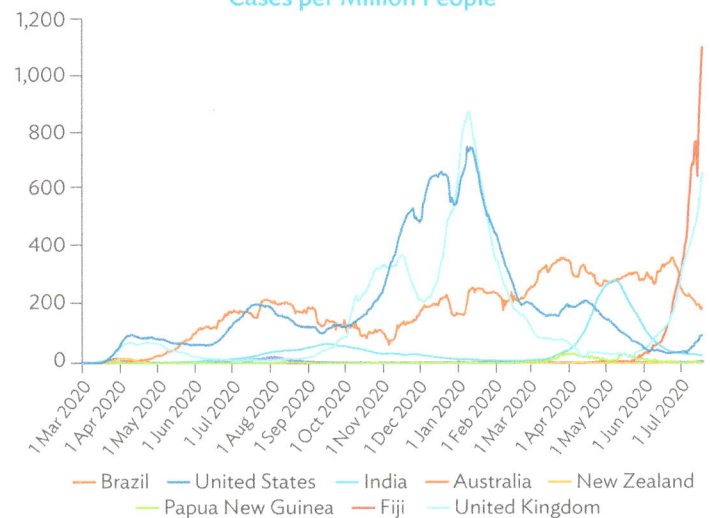

Figure 4: Daily New Confirmed COVID-19 Cases per Million People

COVID-19 = coronavirus disease.
Notes:
1. Data as of 18 July 2021.
2. Cases are based on the rolling 7-day average.
3. The number of confirmed cases is lower than the number of actual cases mainly due to limited testing.
Source: Johns Hopkins University CSSE. 2021. *COVID-19 Data Repository.* https://github.com/CSSEGISandData/COVID-19 (accessed 19 July 2021).

Fiji's national 7-day average test positivity rate[5] is rising and was recorded at 24.0% on 18 July 2021, way higher than the WHO threshold of 5%, indicating widespread community transmission and suggesting that the virus is spreading faster than the growth seen in confirmed cases. The country's two major hospitals were compromised in early May and June, as COVID-19 cases were detected among hospital personnel. As a result, temporary health care facilities were set up to treat non–COVID-19 cases, and the Fiji Emergency Medical Assistance Team[6] was activated. As the number of daily cases approached 200, Fiji called on the emergency medical teams (EMTs) of Australia and New Zealand, a situation that has only taken place in case of disaster emergencies.

Within the health ministry, medical personnel positioned in different areas in the country were reassigned, while medical and dental students in their final year were deployed to augment personnel and private doctors were outsourced to provide free medical services. A hospital ship was also used for certain surgical procedures.

Drawing from experience over the previous year, health authorities enforced localized lockdowns to limit movements to non-containment zones while the government, along with several nongovernment organizations, provided for the basic needs of households within containment zones. However, based on the COVID-19 stringency index (Figure 5), the restrictions imposed during the current outbreak are not as severe as a year ago.

Figure 5: Fiji COVID-19 Stringency Index

COVID-19 = coronavirus disease.
Notes:
1. Data as of 28 June 2021.
2. The stringency index is a composite measure based on nine response indicators including school closures, workplace closures, and travel bans, rescaled to a value from 0 to 100 (100 = strictest).
3. If policies vary at the subnational level, the index is shown as the response level of the strictest subregion.
Source: T. Hale, N. Angrist, R. Goldszmidt , B. Kira , A. Petherick, T. Phillips, S. Webster, E. Cameron-Blake, L. Hallas, S. Majumdar, and H. Tatlow. 2021. "A global panel database of pandemic policies (Oxford COVID-19 Government Response Tracker)." *Nature Human Behaviour*. https://doi.org/10.1038/s41562-021-01079-8 (accessed 7 July 2021).

THE GOVERNMENT'S CURRENT STRATEGY TO COMBAT THE OUTBREAK

As the economic costs increased with the prolonged lockdown, restrictions within containment zones have been eased but with increased surveillance and protocol requirements. For instance, many retailers and businesses are allowed to open but shoppers are required to download a mobile application[7] that will assist authorities in contact tracing, apart from physical distancing, temperature checks, and wearing of masks. With experience from managing disasters triggered by natural hazards' emergencies, the government also uses geographic information system technology to inform the public of the approximate location of new positive cases.

The government has continued supporting those unemployed because of the pandemic by topping up their withdrawable pension funds if they have exhausted a certain portion of their superannuation savings.[8] For those in the informal sector, the government has collaborated with mobile telecommunication companies to provide cash support, first of F$90 per household and later two rounds of F$50 per individual. The cash support is deposited in customers' e-wallets. So far more than 250,000 Fijians have benefitted. In the recent FY2021-2022 budget announcement, the government has set aside an additional F$200 million in unemployment support over the next 6 months (F$120 per month per person) to qualifying individuals in the formal and informal sectors. The government targets to assist 300,000 Fijians in this initiative.

ECONOMIC IMPACT AND FOREGONE OPPORTUNITY[9]

Before the current outbreak, a survey conducted by the Fiji Bureau of Statistics showed that 94% of businesses were adversely affected by the pandemic.[10] 87% of respondents reported declines in business income and, to minimize expenditures, businesses had to renegotiate building rentals and deferment of loan repayments, while also cutting salaries and wages. 59% of enterprises placed staff on temporarily reduced working hours. In addition, 35% reported reduction in capital investment, while 23% and 4% had to defer and cancel capital investments, respectively. About 90% of enterprises reported a decline in revenues while 14% had to close outlets. By industry, the tourism and related sectors were most affected. The second wave is likely to further complicate businesses recovery efforts.

Despite the prolonged closure of international borders, business sentiment had been slowly improving before the current COVID-19 outbreak as enterprises adapted to the "new normal". The Reserve Bank of Fiji's December 2020 biannual business expectations survey noted a net 7% of respondents expected business conditions to deteriorate in the coming 6 months, only a quarter of the proportion in the June 2020 survey. 35% of respondents expected business conditions to improve in the next 12 months compared with 27% in the previous survey.

MITIGATING FISCAL AND HEALTH RISKS

Because of the significant fall in government revenues on an annual basis, with tourism losses wiping out almost one-third of revenues, the government cannot avoid taking on new debt. The current COVID-19 crisis necessitates higher spending on the health and social sectors, with expenditure consolidation in other areas unlikely to make up the gap. Any premature withdrawal of fiscal support is also likely to be counterproductive.

For FY2021 (ends 31 July 2021), the budget shortfall (gross deficit) was equivalent to 27.8% of GDP (if debt repayments are excluded, the net deficit was equivalent to 20.2% of GDP), of which 14.2% of GDP is programmed to be financed by external borrowings. Multilateral partners have provided budget support and technical assistance to promote a private sector-led recovery. Other areas of assistance are to raise productivity and to streamline government fiscal exposure related to state-owned enterprises.

As a part of prudent fiscal management, it is imperative that government-guaranteed debt (equal to 10.4% of GDP as of April 2021) is appropriately managed. High-risk enterprises may need financial assistance in the downside scenario. In the long term, the government could review requirements for guarantees so as not to burden public finances. For short-term interventions, the government needs to manage this carefully and transparently. Towards this end, the government may need to review its current debt management strategy to ensure a downward debt trajectory in the medium term.

CHARTING A COURSE THROUGH THE STORM

The government's current strategy focusses primarily on vaccination, while managing risks and slowing (rather than eliminating) transmission. In this regard, as of 20 July 2021, 70.0% of the eligible population had been vaccinated with one dose of COVID-19 vaccines while 14.3% had been fully vaccinated. The government aims to fully vaccinate the eligible population by October 2021 but a persistent push is required to cover people in remote areas and those who may be currently uncertain about taking the vaccine.

Even if Fiji fully vaccinates its eligible population, opening of the borders for tourism resumption may still take some time. The vaccination rates are relatively low in its traditional tourism markets of Australia and New Zealand. Fiji may consider opening its borders to countries with high vaccination rates first. As of 20 July, these alternative markets with high vaccination rates include North America and Europe (Figure 6).

Figure 6: Share of People Vaccinated Against COVID-19

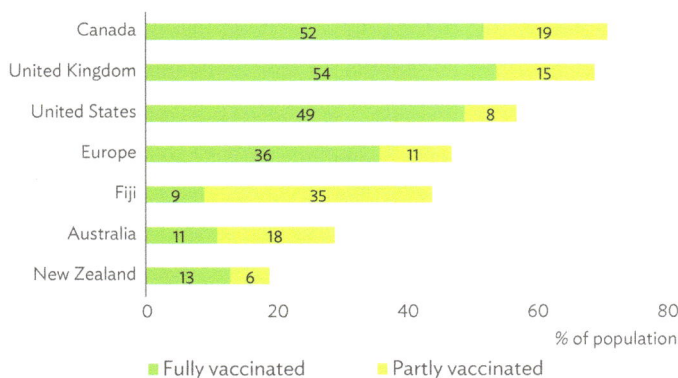

Notes:
1. Data as of 20 July 2021.
2. These data are only available for countries which report the breakdown of doses administered by first and second doses.
3. Based on Fiji's target population (18 years and above), 70.0% have received at least one dose of vaccine while 14.3% have been fully vaccinated as of 20 July 2021 (Government of Fiji, 2021).
Source: Our World in Data. 2021. https://ourworldindata.org/covid-vaccinations (accessed 21 July 2021).

To assess the benefits of this strategy, the following three scenarios were considered. Under a baseline scenario, the average monthly arrivals so far in 2021 (1,259 up to April) are assumed to be sustained until the end of the year. Under this scenario, GDP will further contract by 5.0% this year and recover by 8.8% in 2022. Taking the optimistic

scenario where borders open from November 2021 to countries with high vaccination rates but at only 20% of the comparable figures in 2019,[11] the economy will contract by 4.5% this year but recover by 16.8% next year. Most of the tourist arrivals are assumed to come from North America and Europe as Australia and New Zealand are assumed to open their borders from the second half of 2022. A pessimistic scenario assumes that Fiji will wait for its traditional source countries to make the first move. As such, the scenario assumes zero tourist arrivals for the remainder of 2021 and the first half of 2022 because of the worsening health crisis with borders opening only from the second half of 2022, but at a gradual pace from all source markets. In this case, the economy contracts by 8.5% in 2021, but recovers to 10.4% in 2022.

Compared to pre-pandemic levels, GDP remains 13 percentage points under the baseline scenario, 15 percentage points under the pessimistic scenario, and 6 percentage points under the optimistic scenario (Figure 7). While the optimistic scenario does not fully take GDP to pre-pandemic levels, it minimizes the economic contraction compared to the other scenarios.

Figure 7: Fiji Distance from Pre-pandemic GDP Level

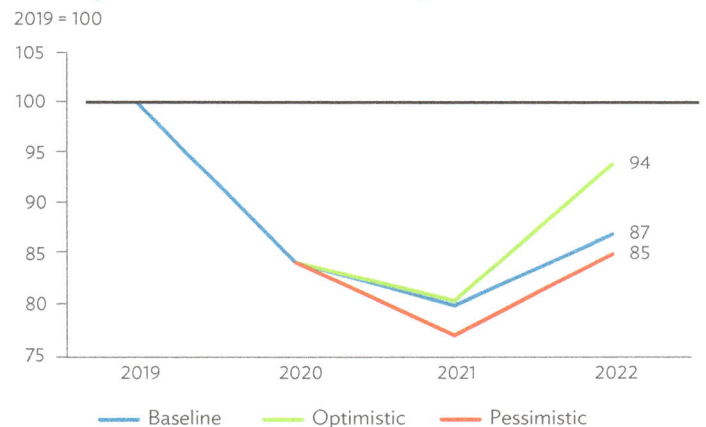

Note: Years refer to fiscal years ended 31 July.
Sources: Government of Fiji and ADB estimates.

This assessment does not include the health implications the strategy might have for society. Given the high incidence of NCDs which increase the risk of hospitalization and severe cases of COVID-19, the health implications may be substantial compared with economic benefits.

In the short run, the government will need to take on more debt to meet immediate financing needs, but a clear strategy is needed to ensure fiscal consolidation in the medium term. For now, expenditure decisions need to focus on priority versus non-priority spending allocations. The government is freezing civil service recruitment for now, and greater effort would be needed to identify and eliminate non-essential spending to allow more space within the existing fiscal envelope. While vaccination can lower the health costs of the pandemic and facilitate economic recovery, in the long term, Fiji still needs to deliver critical reforms to put the economy on a firmer footing.

Endnotes

[1]   The central bank estimates that tourism industry brought in F$1 billion in government revenue in 2019. Based on FY2021 government budget, the revenue collected in 2019 was F$3.2 billion.

[2]   This is based on cause-specific proportional mortality which, according to the report, measures the relative burden of NCDs compared to other causes of deaths.

[3]   There have been 3,697 recoveries in the current wave.

[4]   While the Pacific subregion only pertains to ADB's Pacific developing member countries, Australia and New Zealand are included in these data.

[5]   Calculated as the number of positive tests divided by the number of tests. The WHO had set criteria in May 2020 that, if the ratio is above 5.0%, the outbreak is classified as being out of control. A high ratio indicates either a high number of positive cases or a low number of tests, and indicates higher community transmission among those who have not been tested.

[6]   An initiative of the WHO, EMTs are groups of health professionals that treat patients affected by a disaster or emergency. Currently, there are 25 EMTS globally and Fiji was the 26th member given international recognition, a first in the Pacific apart from Australia and New Zealand. The Fiji Emergency Medical Assistance Team is categorized as a "Type 1 Fixed Emergency Medical Team" and is able to provide a broad range of medical and emergency services for up to 100 patients per day, operating from a fixed structure (commonly referred to as a field hospital), providing up to 12 hours of care per day, 7 days a week. Fiji received this recognition in 2019, boosting efforts to respond to emergency in the Pacific.

[7]   careFIJI is a mobile application by the Government of Fiji to streamline and speed up the Ministry of Health and Medical Services' contact tracing efforts. Using Bluetooth technology that does not capture location or Global Positioning System information, it is based on the TraceTogether mobile application developed by the Government of Singapore and mirrors the COVIDSAFE application widely used in Australia.

[8]   Affected employee drawdown part of their superannuation funds (general balance) first. The government will only top up those who do not have sufficient general account balance. By construction, 30% of superannuation contributions are in a general account with possible withdrawals for life-cycle events, while the rest is kept in a preserved account specifically for retirement purposes.

[9]   The Government of Fiji released its FY2021-2022 National Budget on 16 July 2021, estimating a net deficit of 16.2% of GDP for FY2022, up from a revised deficit of 11.5% of GDP in the last fiscal year. Consequently, government debt is projected to be about 91.6% of GDP by the end of the financial year, from 79.2% in the previous year. The economy is now estimated to have contracted by 15.7% in 2020 (compared to government forecast of -19.0% from November 2020). The government forecast further contraction of 4.1% in 2021 (compared with the earlier forecast of a recovery between 1.6% and 8.0%) because of the current local outbreak.

[10]   The survey, conducted through telephone interviews, targeted businesses that earns more than F$8 million a year. A total of 236 enterprises were surveyed and they contribute more than 70% of total gross output in the economy. The survey was conducted between 25 January 2021 and 12 February 2021, with 90% response rate.

[11]   The conservative estimate is based on the recent experience in the quarantine-free travel bubble between the Cook Islands and New Zealand.

References

Government of Fiji, Fiji Bureau of Statistics; and the Pacific Community. 2019. *Vital Statistics Report 2012–2017*. Suva.

Government of Fiji. 2020. *Economic and Fiscal Update Supplement to the 2020–2021 Budget Address*. Suva.

Government of Fiji. 2021. *Economic and Fiscal Update Supplement to the 2021-2022 Budget Address*. Suva.

Reserve Bank of Fiji. 2021. *The Role of Tourism in Fiji's Post COVID-19 Economic Recovery*. Suva.

Reserve Bank of Fiji. 2021. Understanding Government Debt. Reserve Bank of Fiji newspaper articles. Suva.

Navigating recovery in Kiribati and Tuvalu: strategic fiscal policy and development support

Lead authors: Noel Del Castillo, Lily Anne Homasi, Rommel Rabanal, and Isoa Wainiqolo

The populations of Kiribati and Tuvalu are potentially highly susceptible to coronavirus disease (COVID-19) because of scarce health facilities and a high incidence of preexisting health conditions. Adult obesity, for example, is well above the world average of 13%: at 52% in Tuvalu and 46% in Kiribati. There is mounting evidence of a link between obesity and worse health consequences from COVID-19. Further, half of adults in these two island states use tobacco or double the global average of 24% (World Health Organization 2020).

Geographic isolation and population dispersion, long regarded as constraints on development, and quick government action to close borders have sheltered these two economies from the direct impact of COVID-19, and so they have not suffered the severe effects experienced by other tourist-dependent economies in the Pacific. Nonetheless, their lack of economic diversification contributed to a deterioration in the economies of both countries in 2020. Recovery is expected to take hold gradually, with Tuvalu expected to show faster recovery than Kiribati.

COVID-19 PREPAREDNESS AND RESPONSE PACKAGES

The governments of Kiribati and Tuvalu have both introduced large packages to mitigate the impact of COVID-19 on their economies. These packages, which included financial and technical support from development partners, were used to meet costs associated with health preparedness and to strengthen weak health systems. The health-related expenditure items in the COVID-19 response packages of these countries already account for half of the pre-pandemic budget allocated to their respective health ministries.

In 2020, the Government of Kiribati allocated a budget for its COVID-19 response package equivalent to 4.9% of gross domestic product (GDP) while the Government of Tuvalu, with support from key development partners, spent an equivalent of 10.4% of GDP for COVID-19-related expenditures. These packages, including financial and technical support from development partners, were necessary to meet the cost of health preparedness and to support vulnerable groups. They imposed additional burdens on the finances of these countries, however, and stretched their relatively weak public financial management systems. As these small economies gear up for recovery, a challenge is to deploy these scarce public resources judiciously. Using them to pursue long-term development goals can offer strategic advantages to countries with limited resources.

In both countries, the response packages allocated spending to social protection and support for businesses using funds from fishing license revenues, development partners, and, in Kiribati, the Revenue Equalization Reserve Fund. Tuvalu's social protection program initially included a monthly cash payment to every citizen, but was later amended to target only those unemployed as a result of the pandemic. While universal cash payments are costly, governments sometimes opt for them, especially in the midst of a crisis, if the risk of exclusion error is high.

As governments roll out their response packages and recovery plans, they need to balance people's immediate needs with investments that optimize development impacts of limited resources over the long term. While sharply increased government spending is warranted in a crisis, prudent fiscal management over the medium term should be a guiding principle. Unfettered spending can threaten the sustainability of scarce public resources in Tuvalu. Meanwhile, Kiribati still needs to ensure that its healthy cash balance supports long-term investment with solid development outcomes. Some capital expenditures, such as aircraft and ship purchases, must be carefully considered, as they may have long-term fiscal implications in terms of resources for operation and maintenance, subsidies, and associated infrastructure which potentially outweigh the benefits.

The role of development partners, both in the preparation and recovery stages, cannot be overstated. Given the generally weak health systems in these countries, support from development partners has been vital to prevent, detect, and respond to the threat posed by COVID-19. ADB has extended a $1.5 million grant to the Government of Kiribati and a $630,000 grant to the Government of Tuvalu to defray the provision of personal protective equipment for COVID-19 preparedness and response, recruitment of health workers and payment of overtime for essential workforce; transportation and logistics, and costs related to quarantining of suspected or confirmed COVID-19 patients (ADB 2020a, 2020b). Similar grants were extended by the World Bank to both Kiribati and Tuvalu totaling $2.5 million each to strengthen its public health preparedness efforts and respond to urgent needs created by the pandemic (World Bank 2020a, 2020b).

PATH TO RECOVERY

Through the global COVAX Facility (a partnership among the Coalition for Epidemic Preparedness Innovations, Gavi, UNICEF, and the World Health Organization), both Kiribati and Tuvalu have received doses of COVID-19 vaccines sufficient to cover up to 20% of the eligible population. Both countries have also received additional vaccine doses and vaccine rollout support through bilateral partners, including the governments of Australia and New Zealand. With a COVID-19 vaccination program that began in April, Tuvalu has reached 40% coverage of the target population with the first dose of the vaccine. Kiribati's vaccination program started in late May, and has so far covered 12% of the 20% population. Tuvalu has signed a $1.5 million grant agreement with ADB to further support the rollout of COVID-19 vaccine and associated strengthening to the immunization program (upgrading of cold chain capacities, training of health workers, and community engagement). This grant is additional financing to the existing System Strengthening for Effective Coverage of New Vaccines in the Pacific Project approved by ADB in 2018.

More than a year after the pandemic started, governments have started outlining their recovery plans to prepare for the eventual reopening of the global economy. In Kiribati, the government is expected to spend equivalent to 100% of GDP this year, with the education and health sectors getting the biggest shares in recurrent spending (Government of Kiribati 2020b). Recurrent spending, inclusive of COVID-19 response programs, is budgeted to increase to the equivalent of 93% of GDP in 2021, from 86% in 2020 and below 70% prior to the pandemic (Figure 8). Rising recurrent spending partly offsets compressed capital outlays—largely reflecting delays in implementation of development partner-funded projects—which have averaged only about 7.3% of GDP in 2020–2021, from a pre-pandemic average of 33.6%. Although part of its budget has been earmarked for COVID-19-related spending, it is also guided by its long-term development plan, the Kiribati 20-Year Vision 2016–2036, which focuses on the development of its fisheries and tourism sectors.

Figure 8: Kiribati: Components of Government Expenditure

% of GDP

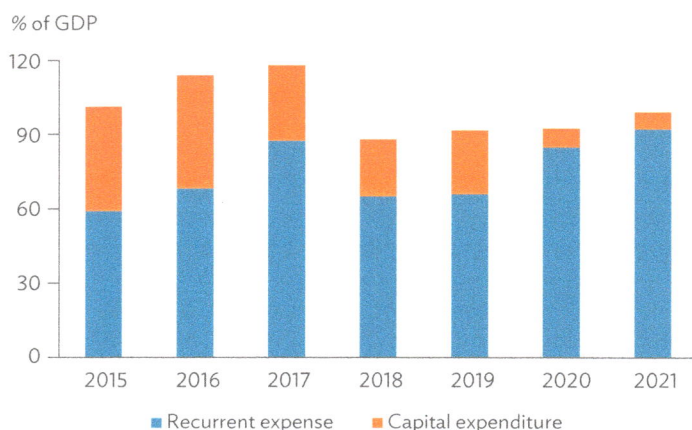

GDP = gross domestic product.
Sources: Kiribati National Budget 2021; and Asian Development Outlook and Pacific Economic Monitor databases.

Meanwhile, the Government of Tuvalu passed its 2021 budget with expenditures equivalent to 160.8% of GDP (Government of Tuvalu 2020). It coincides with its new national strategy for sustainable development 2021–2030, *Te Kete*, targeting key areas such as sea and air transport and strengthening internet connectivity. Similarly, recurrent spending is budgeted to increase further to 128% of GDP in 2021, from 123% in 2020—largely reflecting COVID-19 response measures—from an already high pre-pandemic average of 99% of GDP, given the economy's small size even relative to other Pacific island economies (Figure 9). The 2021 budget plans for a ramping up in capital spending to the equivalent of 33% of GDP, close to the pre-pandemic average of 37%, after project implementation delays limited outlays to 12% of GDP in 2020. However, such a ramping up will depend heavily on progress to implement measures for safe and gradual reopening.

Two important sources of financing for these two countries, aside from taxes, are fishing licenses and earnings from their respective sovereign wealth funds. Prudent use of these resources is always

desired, considering the volatile nature of the fisheries sector and the sustainability concern over public trust funds.

Figure 9: Tuvalu: Components of Government Expenditure

% of GDP

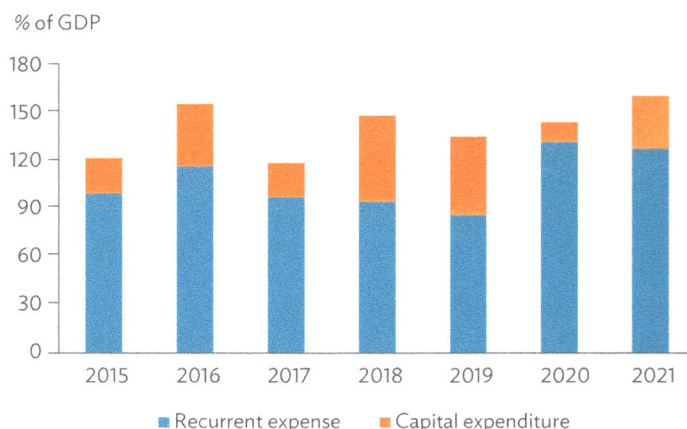

GDP = gross domestic product.
Sources: Tuvalu National Budget 2021; and Asian Development Outlook and Pacific Economic Monitor databases.

Given the narrow economic bases of Kiribati and Tuvalu, financial support provided by development partners will play an important role to boost recovery. The Government of Kiribati is expected to receive budget support in 2021 equivalent to 5.1% of GDP. The support for recurrent budget will be provided by the European Union, the World Bank, and the governments of Australia and New Zealand. Meanwhile, the development budget of Kiribati will receive funding from ADB, the European Union, the World Bank, United Nations (UN) agencies,[1] and bilateral support from the governments of Australia, Japan, the People's Republic of China, New Zealand, and Taipei,China (Government of Kiribati 2020b, 2020c). On the other hand, the Government of Tuvalu is expecting funding from development partners of up to 51.4% of GDP, subject to confirmation (Government of Tuvalu 2019, 2020). The Government of Tuvalu is discussing the details of budgetary support with the World Bank, ADB, the European Union, and the governments of Australia, New Zealand, and Taipei,China. Tuvalu's development projects for 2021 will be financed by multilateral organizations such as ADB, the European Union, the Pacific Community, the World Bank, and UN agencies;[2] bilateral assistance from the governments of Australia, India, Italy, New Zealand, the Republic of Korea, Taipei,China, and the United States; and nongovernment organizations which include the Green Climate Fund, the Global Fund, and the Global Environment Facility (Government of Tuvalu, 2019).

Development partner support has also come in the form of programs that will directly address a specific concern or assessments that will provide information to help policymakers on the best course of action. For instance, in Kiribati, the United Nations' COVID-19 Response and Recovery Multi-Partner Trust Fund will support small-scale fisheries and aquaculture production as well as small-scale agriculture production systems, micronutrient supplementation and nutrition counseling for pregnant and breastfeeding women, and capacity-building for health workers. Meanwhile, in Tuvalu, the COVID-19 Response and Recovery Multi-Partner Trust Fund is funding the International Organization for Migration and the International Labour Organization in partnership with the Government of Tuvalu to assess the impacts of COVID-19 on Tuvaluan households, workers, and businesses.

CONCLUDING REMARKS

The COVID-19 response provides opportunities to pursue strategic reform that improves public financial management, and address short- and long-term challenges. The additional financing by development partners has helped Kiribati and Tuvalu avoid making significant cutbacks in other expenditures. As these countries navigate toward economic recovery, the challenge of managing this funding is how to utilize it strategically to magnify the benefits of its plans and broaden its scope to include long-term goals.

In this regard, governments may consider strengthening primary health-care services as part of their recovery plans. Beyond COVID-19 response, this would better enable them to handle general public health concerns and noncommunicable "lifestyle" diseases. Improving facilities in satellite health clinics, for example, can ease the burden on larger hospitals, allowing them to focus more on curative care. The main hospitals in these countries are generally in disrepair and struggle to deliver basic services. They and the people they serve would benefit from increased investment and operational funding to strengthen health-care services.

Endnotes

[1] The UN agencies supporting Kiribati include the Food and Agriculture Organization, the United Nations Children's Emergency Fund, the United Nations Development Programme, the UN Environment Programme, the United Nations Population Fund, the UN Women, and the World Health Organization.

[2] The UN agencies supporting Tuvalu include the United Nations Capital Development Fund, the United Nations Development Programme, the UN Environment Programme, and the United Nations Population Fund.

References

ADB. 2018. *Grant Agreement (Systems Strengthening for Effective Vaccine Coverage of New Vaccines in the Pacific Project) Between Tuvalu and Asian Development Bank.* https://www.adb.org/sites/default/files/project-documents/50282/50282-001-grj-en_0.pdf.

ADB. 2020a. *Grant Agreement Between Republic of Kiribati and Asian Development Bank.* https://www.adb.org/sites/default/files/project-documents/54135/54135-003-grj-en_7.pdf.

ADB. 2020b. *Grant Agreement Between Tuvalu and Asian Development Bank.* https://www.adb.org/sites/default/files/project-documents/54135/54135-003-grj-en_0.pdf.

ADB. 2021a. *Asian Development Outlook: Financing a Green and Inclusive Recovery.* Manila.

ADB. 2021b. *Grant Agreement Between Tuvalu and Asian Development Bank.* https://www.adb.org/sites/default/files/project-documents/50282/50282-003-grj-en.pdf.

Government of Kiribati. 2018. *2019 Budget: Investing in Inclusive Development.* Tarawa.

Government of Kiribati. 2020a. *2020 Recurrent Budget: Elevating Kiribati to Greater Prosperity.* Tarawa.

Government of Kiribati. 2020b. *2021 Recurrent Budget: Embracing the New Normal.* Tarawa.

Government of Kiribati. 2020c. *2021 Development Budget: Embracing the New Normal.* Tarawa.

Government of Tuvalu. 2019. *2020 National Budget.* Funafuti.

Government of Tuvalu. 2019. *Tuvalu Development Fund Estimates 2020.* Funafuti.

Government of Tuvalu. 2020. *2021 National Budget.* Funafuti.

International Organization for Migration. 2021. Bolstering Tuvalu's Socioeconomic Resilience in a COVID-19 World. https://www.iom.int/news/bolstering-tuvalus-socioeconomic-resilience-covid-19-world. News release. 30 March.

United Nations. 2020. *Enhancing Food Security, Nutrition, and Resilience in Kiribati.* http://mptf.undp.org/factsheet/project/00121737.

World Bank. 2020a. COVID-19 Prevention Drives Boost for Public Health in Kiribati. https://www.worldbank.org/en/news/press-release/2020/06/26/covid-19-prevention-drives-boost-for-public-health-in-kiribati. News release. 26 June.

World Bank. 2020b. Tuvalu - Maritime Investment in Climate Resilient Operations Project - Additional Financing. https://www.worldbank.org/en/news/loans-credits/2020/06/05/tuvalu-maritime-investment-in-climate-resilient-operations-project-additional-financing-covid-19-coronavirus. News release. 5 June.

World Health Organization. *The Global Health Observatory (database).* https://www.who.int/data/gho (accessed 20 June 2020).

World Health Organization. 2021a. Kiribati receives 24,000 doses of COVID-19 vaccines through the COVAX Facility. https://www.who.int/westernpacific/about/how-we-work/pacific-support/news/detail/25-05-2021-kiribati-receives-24-000-doses-of-covid-19-vaccines-through-the-covax-facility. News release. 25 May.

World Health Organization. 2021b. Tuvalu receives 4,800 doses of COVID-19 vaccines through the COVAX facility. https://www.who.int/westernpacific/about/how-we-work/pacific-support/news/detail/08-04-2021-tuvalu-receives-4-800-doses-of-covid-19-vaccines-through-the-covax-facility. News release. 8 April.

Cautious steps toward reopening in the Federated States of Micronesia and the Marshall Islands

Lead authors: Remrick Patagan and Cara Tinio

The Federated States of Micronesia (FSM) and the Marshall Islands, as well as Palau, are benefitting from early access to coronavirus disease (COVID-19) vaccines through Operation Warp Speed of the United States (US). These countries commenced their national vaccination programs in early 2021, but progress to-date has varied because of various factors, most notably geographic dispersion of populations, capacity of health systems, and vaccine hesitancy (Figure 10).

Figure 10: Fully Vaccinated People
(% of adult population)

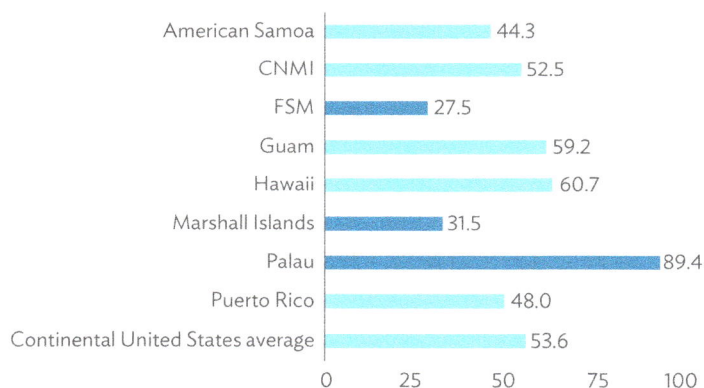

American Samoa	44.3
CNMI	52.5
FSM	27.5
Guam	59.2
Hawaii	60.7
Marshall Islands	31.5
Palau	89.4
Puerto Rico	48.0
Continental United States average	53.6

CNMI = Commonwealth of the Northern Mariana Islands, FSM = Federated States of Micronesia.
Note: Data as of 13 June 2021.
Source: US Center for Disease Control Vaccine Tracking System (accessed 13 June 2021).

While timely border closures limited the North Pacific economies' direct exposure to COVID-19—indeed, all cases recorded in these countries have been historical cases detected at the border (Table 1)—vaccination remains key to economic reopening and revival. This article examines the latest steps taken by the FSM and the Marshall Islands toward safe reopening of borders and commencing recovery from the pandemic's deep economic and social impacts. (A discussion on Palau's reopening in the context of quarantine-free travel is on page 5.)

Table 1: COVID-19 Cases in the North Pacific

Country	Active Cases	Recovered	Deaths
Federated States of Micronesia	0	1	0
Marshall Islands	0	4	0
Palau	0	2	0

COVID-19 = coronavirus disease.
Notes: Data as of 15 July 2021. All cases recorded in the North Pacific are classified as historical cases.
Sources: M. Roser, H. Ritchie, E. Ortiz-Ospina, and J. Hasell. 2020. Coronavirus Pandemic (COVID-19). Published online at OurWorldInData.org. Retrieved from: https://ourworldindata.org/coronavirus [Online Resource]; Palau Ministry of Health. 2021. Coronavirus Disease 2019 (COVID-19) Situation Report. Retrieved from: https://web.archive.org/web/20210613161725/ http://www.palauhealth.org/2019nCoV_SitRep/MOH-COVID-19%20Situation%20Report.pdf.

FEDERATED STATES OF MICRONESIA: BROADENING VACCINE OUTREACH AND SOCIAL PROTECTION

FSM's COVID-19 vaccination program started in January 2021 through Operation Warp Speed and was initially rolled out among frontline workers, the elderly, and those with underlying conditions. In February, vaccination was made available to the rest of the adult population (residents 18 years old and above) and coverage has been steadily increasing. The country aims to vaccinate 70% of adults before repatriating citizens from areas affected by COVID-19.

As of 10 July, 46.9% of the adult population had been fully vaccinated with varying rates of coverage per state (Table 2). According to the US Health Resources & Services Administration's *Health Center COVID-19 Survey Summary Report*, the primary logistics challenges in COVID-19 vaccination in the FSM are staffing for vaccine administration and storage capacity.

Table 2: Federated States of Micronesia Vaccination Coverage, by State

State	% Fully Vaccinated (among 18 years old and above)
Yap	56.8
Chuuk	41.0
Kosrae	49.4
Pohnpei	58.5
National average	46.9

Note: Data as of 10 July 2021.
Source: Federated States of Micronesia, Department of Health and Social Affairs. 2021. *FSM COVID-19 Vaccination*. https://hsa.gov.fm/fsm-covid-19-vaccination/.

The government has been exploring ways to improve vaccination coverage, particularly in outlying lagoon islands and remote villages. The FSM has requested the US Center for Disease Control and Prevention for more single-dose Johnson & Johnson vaccines, which have less stringent logistics requirements than the

Moderna and Pfizer-BioNTech vaccines, and the US Coast Guard for assistance in repatriation of patients and attendants, as well as diplomats and medical professionals to assist with vaccinations and training.

In response, the US Coast Guard conducted two flights on 13–14 May 2021 repatriating FSM citizens and delivering US and foreign diplomats from Guam to Pohnpei International Airport. These were the first flights received by the country since it closed international borders in March 2020. Reflecting the country's cautious approach to gradual reopening, all passengers were fully vaccinated, underwent pre-travel quarantine, and tested negative for COVID-19. Preparations are underway for bringing back FSM citizens from neighboring Palau and the Marshall Islands, which have also remained free of local COVID-19 transmission.

In addition, the FSM President raised the possibility of tying financial assistance payments with proof of vaccination. On 8 June, the government launched the Low-Income Assistance Program in partnership with ADB, which provided funding support for the program. The cash transfers for low-income households focus on informal sector workers who do not qualify for unemployment assistance from the US Department of Labor. Meanwhile, assistance to vulnerable groups includes temporary waivers of medical expenses not included in US funding under the Compact of Free Association, electricity subsidies for low-income families with dependents with disabilities, solar lamps for remote areas, and measures against gender-based violence.

These assistance measures seek to fill gaps in existing social safety nets, support household financial balances, and in turn reduce long-term economic scarring. All of the above will be important in paving the way for a quick recovery once reopening of international borders and easing of public health restrictions proceed in earnest.

MARSHALL ISLANDS: REVIVING ACTIVITY IN FISHERIES

The Marshall Islands' Majuro port is a major mid-Pacific hub for the purse seine fishery and was the world's busiest tuna transshipment port in FY2014–FY2019 (ended 30 September), averaging more than 500 transshipments a year that moved more than 355,500 metric tons of tuna to offshore canneries (Figure 11). This has helped generate businesses providing complementary onshore services, such as net repair and supply provisioning, and drive related manufacturing activities; and earned the Marshall Islands more than $605,000 a year in transshipment revenues.

The recent pickup in transshipment activity stalled in early 2020 when the Marshall Islands imposed border restrictions at the onset of the COVID-19 pandemic. A 14-day isolation requirement for vessels seeking to enter Majuro lagoon, together with limits on the number of them that can be in the transshipment area at a time, diverted vessels to ports with fewer entry restrictions. This resulted in just 180 tuna transshipments in Majuro port for all of 2020, followed by an average of just 11 per month in January–April 2021 (Figure 12).

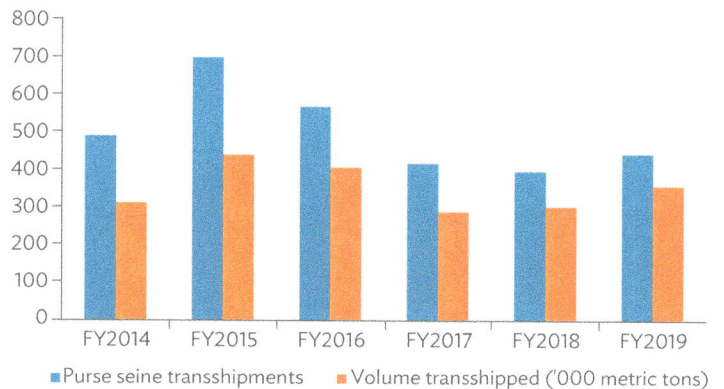

Figure 11: Tuna Transshipment Activity in Majuro Port, Marshall Islands

FY = fiscal year.
Note: Fiscal year ends 30 September of that year.
Sources: Marshall Islands Marine Resources Authority. *Annual Report*. Majuro (7 years: FY2013–FY2019).

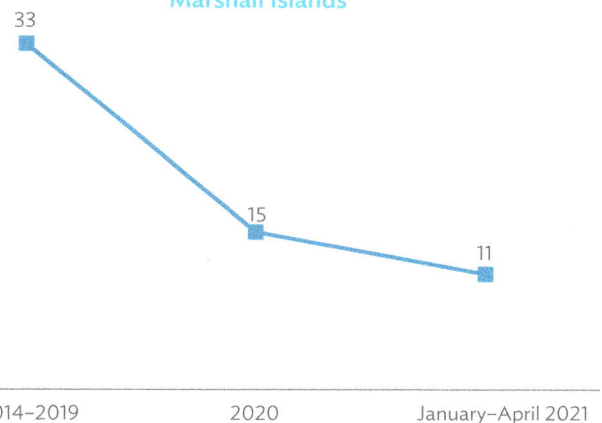

Figure 12: Average Monthly Transshipments in Majuro Port, Marshall Islands

Note: Numbers reported suggest that this is on a calendar year basis.
Source: ADB estimates based on Radio New Zealand. 2021. Tuna transshipment in Majuro shows first sign of rebound. 10 June.

Besides directly depressing transshipment revenues, the diminished activity also affected local fuel sales and other onshore fishing-related business activity in Majuro. Further, fisheries observers—previously required on all purse seine vessels to ensure effective surveillance and control of tuna stocks—were pulled out to minimize potentially risky contact and promote social distancing, drying up observer fee revenues that had amounted to almost $694,000 a year in FY2014–FY2019.

On 29 April, the Marshall Islands released Travel Issuance No. 25 removing the quarantine requirement for fishing vessels entering Majuro lagoon, instead requiring clearances to allow port entry. Tuna transshipment activity subsequently picked up in May, with 24 transshipments. Besides being more than double the activity seen in the first 4 months of the year, this total was the highest since the 33 transshipments recorded in December 2019. Twenty-two of the transshipments recorded in May involved transfers from purse seiners to carrier vessels, while two involved unloading the tuna catch into freezer containers at the main commercial dock, entailing some onshore contact.

The following month, the Marshall Islands made COVID-19 vaccinations available on a voluntary basis to commercial fishermen in Majuro port, making the country possibly the first in the Pacific to do so. This follows significant progress made in inoculating the local adult population: 83% and 75% of people aged 18 and above have been fully vaccinated in the Marshall Islands' two urban centers of Kwajalein and Majuro, respectively, as of 7 July, and vaccinations have commenced in the outer islands. Most of the fishermen working on commercial vessels are Asian, with just about 40 Marshallese crew members on all Marshall Islands-registered purse seiners. On 9 June, the first day of this initiative, more than 50 fishermen received the single-dose Johnson & Johnson vaccine. More are expected to be inoculated as fishing vessels continue to call at Majuro port, subject to availability of vaccines.

Besides this ongoing immunization drive, the Ministry of Health and Human Services is working to translate information on COVID-19 prevention into languages that the predominantly Asian crews on these vessels can understand (e.g., Mandarin). It is also planning to roll out the vaccinations for fishermen, currently focused on crews working on purse seine vessels, to longline vessels. There are about 30 longline vessels based locally, also with mostly Asian crews.

CONCLUSION

This article discussed some approaches towards reopening borders amid the continued risk of COVID-19. In preparation for safely repatriating citizens and reintroducing foreign visitors, the FSM is working to extend COVID-19 vaccinations, especially to more remote areas by shifting to more manageable vaccine types and using social protection measures as an incentive to encourage vaccination, among others. Besides continuing with its own vaccine rollout, the Marshall Islands has devoted efforts to safely reopening its fishery sector through a managed reduction of quarantine requirements for fishing vessels and by offering COVID-19 vaccinations to crews.

As vaccine coverage broadens and their populations are more protected from COVID-19, countries have more room to reopen strategic pockets of their economies and jumpstart recovery from the impacts of the pandemic. However, pending further scientific advances in protecting against the disease, continued implementation of public health protocols will remain necessary to contain the risk of transmission. Experiences in reopening parts of the economy, whether locally or from other countries, must be carefully monitored as these can yield valuable lessons for resuming business activity in other sectors even as substantial public health risks persist.

References

Government of the Federated States of Micronesia. 2021. COVID-19 Vaccines Now Available for All Eligible Citizens (18+) in All FSM States. FSM Information Services Press Release. https://gov.fm/index.php/component/content/article/35-pio-articles/news-and-updates/430-covid-19-vaccines-now-available-for-all-eligible-citizens-18-in-all-fsm-states. 22 February.

Government of the Marshall Islands, Ministry of Health and Human Services. RMI COVID-19 Vaccination Rate for 18 Years Old and Above. https://rmihealth.org/ (accessed 12 July 2021).

Graduate School USA. 2020. Assessing the Impact of COVID-19 on the Marshall Islands Economy. https://pitiviti.org/storage/files/econmap/Assessing%20the%20Impact%20of%20COVID-19%20on%20the%20Republic%20of%20the%20Marshall%20Islands.pdf.

Health Resources and Services Administration. 2021. Federated States of Micronesia Health Center COVID-19 Survey Summary Report. https://bphc.hrsa.gov/emergency-response/coronavirus-health-center-data/fm. 4 June.

Marshall Islands Marine Resources Authority. Annual Report. Majuro (7 years: FY2013–FY2019).

Mathieu, E., H. Ritchie, E. Ortiz-Ospina, et al. 2021. A global database of COVID-19 vaccinations. Nature Human Behavior. https://ourworldindata.org/covid-vaccinations.

Maui News. 2021. Coast Guard Conducts Repatriation Flights to Federated States of Micronesia. https://mauinow.com/2021/05/17/coast-guard-conducts-repatriation-flights-to-federated-states-of-micronesia/. 17 May.

Pacific Daily News. 2021. Federated States of Micronesia to assist low-income households. https://www.guampdn.com/story/news/local/2021/02/18/fsm-preparing-give-aid-assist-low-income-households/4499790001/. 19 February.

Pacific Daily News. 2021. Federated States of Micronesia gives COVID-19 vaccine to eligible adults. https://www.guampdn.com/story/news/2021/02/22/federated-states-micronesia-offers-vaccine-adults/4537626001/. 22 February.

Pacific Daily News. 2021. FSM looking at ways to improve COVID-19 vaccination rates. https://www.guampdn.com/story/news/local/2021/03/23/fsm-covid-vaccination-rate-update/6974624002/. 24 March.

Pacific Daily News. 2021. Federated States of Micronesia launches low income social program. https://www.guampdn.com/story/money/2021/06/09/federated-states-micronesia-gives-7-million-low-income-families/7597838002/. 9 June.

Radio New Zealand. 2020. Marshall Islands fisheries revenue expected to drop 20 percent. https://www.rnz.co.nz/international/pacific-news/433528/marshall-islands-fisheries-revenue-expected-to-drop-20-percent. 24 December.

Radio New Zealand. 2021. Tuna transshipment in Majuro shows first sign of rebound. https://www.rnz.co.nz/international/pacific-news/444414/tuna-transshipment-in-majuro-shows-first-sign-of-rebound. 10 June.

Radio New Zealand. 2021. Marshalls vaccinates fishermen in Majuro. https://www.rnz.co.nz/international/pacific-news/444681/marshalls-vaccinates-fishermen-in-majuro. 14 June.

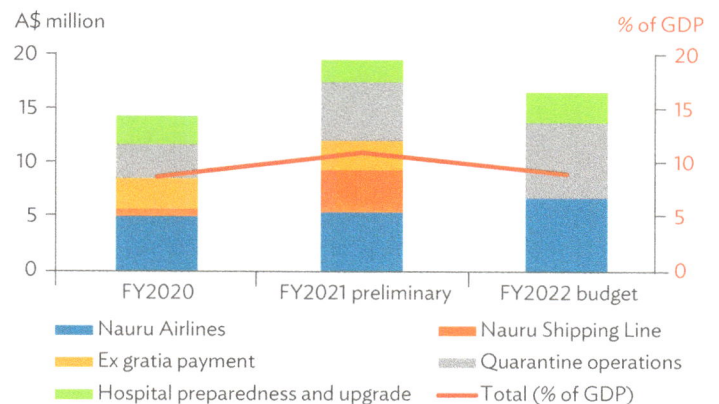

Figure 13: Nauru COVID-19 Expenditure

COVID-19 = coronavirus disease, FY = fiscal year, GDP = gross domestic product.
Source: ADB estimates using data from Nauru budget documents.

Three things that helped Nauru achieve full adult vaccination

Lead author: Prince Cruz

Aside from being one of the remaining few countries free of the coronavirus disease (COVID-19), Nauru is also one of the countries with the highest proportion of its adult population vaccinated against the virus. The country announced that 7,457 people received the first dose while 6,779 got two doses as of 3 July. This corresponds to 109.5% of the country's 6,812 adults (based on the 2019 Census) vaccinated with the first dose, and 99.5% with the second dose.[1] The government said that they will ensure that all eligible adults in Nauru would be fully vaccinated against COVID-19.[2] Here are three things that helped them achieve their targets:

(i) **Small and compact.** With a population of under 12,000 living on a single 21-square kilometer island, the vaccination rollout was done in 1 month for each dose. Being small and compact also helped in fighting vaccine hesitancy. The government coordinated with community and religious leaders to ensure that accurate information was disseminated.

(ii) **Going all out.** The vaccination program is a key element of the government's strategy against COVID-19. Total spending for COVID-19 response was equivalent to 8.8% of gross domestic product (GDP) in fiscal year (FY, ended 30 June) 2020 and 11.0% of GDP in FY2021 (Figure 13). For FY2022, the government has allotted an additional 9.1% of GDP. About one-third of the COVID-19 response (A$10.6 million in FY2020 and FY2021, with an additional A$6.9 million in FY2022) represents subsidies to the state-owned airline, Nauru Air, which has been instrumental in fetching vaccines directly from India.

The vaccination rollout for the first dose was done in 4 weeks from mid-April. The second dose followed in June. Vaccination centers were established in several administrative districts and in the Nauru Ron Hospital, with some remaining open until 7 p.m. Transportation was provided for disadvantaged groups, and walk-ins were allowed for those who missed their schedule or wanted to get their shots earlier.

(iii) **Good development partner relations.** The vaccines received were from Australia through the global vaccine alliance, COVAX (7,200 doses) and India (10,000 doses).[3] Nauru also received financial and administrative support from other development partners for the vaccine rollout, including a grant from ADB's Asia Pacific Disaster Response Fund. Grants rose from the equivalent of 6.1% of GDP in FY2020 to 11.6% of GDP in FY2021. The 2022 budget indicated that grants are seen to fall back to 6.7% of GDP.

Endnotes

[1] Figures from other sources providing data on COVID-19 vaccinations show Nauru at 69.5% as of 20 July 2021 (p. 33). This is based on the vaccine doses as a percent of total population, whereas the government figure is based on doses as a percent of adult population. About 40% of the population is under 18 years old, hence are currently ineligible to receive the Astra Zeneca vaccine in use in Nauru.

[2] Government of Nauru. 2021. *Ten percent to full vaccination*. Nauru Bulletin. Issue 3-2021/228. 9 July 2021. http://naurugov.nr/media/146514/nauru_bulletin___03_9jul2021___228_.pdf

[3] The Government of Nauru initially purchased the vaccines, but it has been fully reimbursed by the Government of Australia as part of its assistance. Government of Nauru. 2021. Australia, India donations of COVID vaccines ensure full coverage. http://naurugov.nr/government-information-office/media-release/australia,-india-donations-of-covid-vaccines-ensure-full-coverage.aspx

Strong public financial management and economic recovery in Papua New Guinea

Lead author: Edward Faber

The coronavirus disease (COVID-19) pandemic has inflicted a heavy shock on the economy of Papua New Guinea (PNG). Based on various estimates, it contracted by 3%–4% in 2020. PNG desperately needs a strong recovery. But the economy, which was already in the doldrums before the pandemic, continues to be extremely weak, not helped by continued persistence of cases of COVID-19 and low rates of vaccination. It increasingly looks as if 2021 may be another year of lost growth. With an election looming in 2022, next year may also be challenging as the effectiveness of the government is weighed down by political concerns.

Fiscal stimulus has been advocated as one approach to support economic recovery; indeed, it has been advanced worldwide by governments seeking to support their economies. However, excessive borrowing within the context of a relatively small developing economy such as PNG can lead to increased macroeconomic challenges and vulnerability and, in a fragile state such as PNG, it also raises questions around how effectively extra borrowings will be spent.

Strong public financial management (PFM) including macro-fiscal management therefore remains of paramount importance for PNG as it charts a path of economic recovery out of the pandemic.

Strengthening domestic resource mobilization lies at the heart of stronger PFM. PNG's tax-to-gross domestic product (GDP) ratio (i.e., total revenues excluding grants and nontax revenues) is low, averaging 14.1% of GDP over the last 5 years. This is below the desired tax yield of 15% of GDP—a level now widely regarded as the minimum required for sustainable development (Gaspar, Jaramillo, and Wingender 2016). Positively, to guide reform, PNG has already developed a Medium-Term Revenue Strategy, 2018–2022 with the assistance of the International Monetary Fund (IMF). This is focused on reforms that improve tax legislation, tax administration, and tax policy. Although the pace of reform has been slow, progress has been made. An IMF Staff Monitored Program, which commenced in February 2020, supports advancing domestic resource mobilization reforms. Such reforms include the passing of a revised Income Tax Act and implementation of a revised Tax Administration Act. The revisions simplify and modernize tax law, replacing earlier legislation that was cumbersome and allowed for concessions, thereby strengthening revenue collection.

Having a strong expenditure framework built around a reliable and credible budget and supported by strong controls is a further essential component of sound PFM. One area where PNG has struggled is with the public sector wage bill, which averaged about one-third of the total expenditure envelope over the last 5 years and has frequently exceeded budget estimates. While this is partly a function of underbudgeting, it is also due to weak payroll controls. To support bringing the public wage bill under greater control, the authorities have begun a payroll cleansing exercise and have

intentions for an independent audit to be conducted, which will help inform future direction in payroll reform.

To strengthen financial controls, PNG has made progress over the last decade with the rolling out of its integrated financial management system (IFMS). The IFMS is an information technology system that enables more accurate recording of financial transactions and improved interface with other government systems, such as the payroll and tax revenue administration systems. Whereas only three ministries were directly linked to IFMS in 2014, by 2021 all national departments were connected. Additionally, 14 of the 22 provinces are now connected, and all provincial health authorities are connected. Ensuring the continued rollout of this system will be essential to ensure strong financial management. This applies particularly to subnational level administrations. Each year the central government allocates funds to provinces and districts through service improvement programs; however, the financial accountability of these funds is limited.

Effective and strong PFM requires the development of sound supporting fiscal strategies and frameworks that are adhered to. PNG successfully developed a Medium-Term Fiscal Strategy (MTFS) in 2017, the third of its kind, seeking fiscal consolidation. However, a change in administration, followed by the COVID-19 pandemic, saw a large departure from the original fiscal framework, with a path taken instead towards wider, less sustainable budget deficits, albeit with an aim to stimulate growth through increased capital expenditure. This trend is set to continue, with the government forecasting deficits equivalent to 7.3% of GDP in 2021 and 5.3% in 2022. It will be important for PNG to swiftly develop a new MTFS, which will be required alongside the next planning cycle. Adhering to such a strategy will gain the confidence of external multilateral and bilateral partners and private sector investors.

In line with this, PNG's fiscal rules need to be carefully reconsidered. The Fiscal Responsibility Act, which sets out key fiscal rules, has been frequently amended over the last 5 years, allowing rules to be increasingly flexible. Such frequent revisions, however, erode confidence. PNG's original ceiling for its debt-to-GDP ratio was 30% (based on the 2006 Fiscal Responsibility Act amendment); however, the upper threshold now stands at 60%. In 2017, a rule requiring that "the budget will be in balance over the term of the government" was replaced with "the government's fiscal strategy will target a zero average annual non-resource primary fiscal balance over the medium term" (where the non-resource primary fiscal balance is defined as the annual net lending or borrowing amount in fiscal accounts adjusted for interest payments and taxes and dividends from mining, petroleum, and gas sectors but does not include expenditure and interest costs from reconstruction and growth debt). However, understanding the calculations behind such a ratio takes time and it may not be quickly understood on the floors of Parliament; further, targets set for this ratio have been missed (Figure 14). PNG's previous MTFS, 2013–2017 set a limit for the annual budget deficit of 2.5% of GDP. Given PNG's current escalation in debt, it may be prudent to consider such a fiscal anchor within PNG's next fiscal strategy, albeit giving some allowance for such a ratio to be exceeded in the event of economic shocks.

Such simple fiscal anchors can be easily understood and followed, which is especially important in the context of PNG's fluid political context. Meanwhile, should PNG experience a tax windfall from rising commodity prices, there will be need for a strategy to pay down debt and operationalize the sovereign wealth fund.

Figure 14: Fiscal Rules in Papua New Guinea

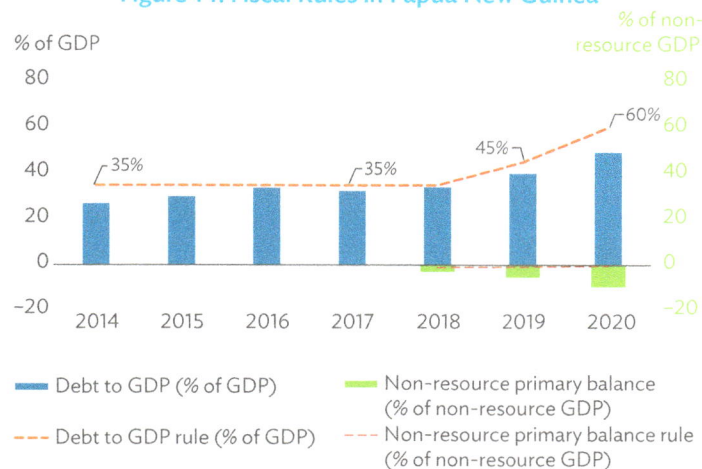

GDP = gross domestic product.
Sources: Government of Papua New Guinea, Fiscal Responsibility Act (as amended, various years); and Government of Papua New Guinea, National Budget Reports (various years).

Strengthened debt management is an important component of strong PFM and is all the more important considering the events of 2020, which resulted in PNG's debt-to-GDP ratio jumping to 49.2% and the IMF changing, in June 2020, its assessment of PNG's debt profile to high risk of debt distress. Recent challenges have included managing rollover risks and incorporating accurate debt data including on contingent liabilities, arrears, and debt related to state-owned enterprises. To strengthen debt management, the government plans to seek and benefit from development partners' capacity building technical assistance to put in place policies and procedures to mitigate debt risks and vulnerabilities.

Strengthening the preparation and publication of financial accounts for public bodies, including state-owned enterprises, statutory bodies, government departments, and provincial and district authorities is greatly needed. Frequently, accounts are not prepared or are many years behind schedule, with no independent audit conducted and with accounts not made public. Strengthening the Auditor-General's Office and wider rollout of the IFMS system for more accurate data capture is therefore needed.

PNG has had four Public Expenditure and Financial Accountability assessments conducted in its history. The most recent was in 2020; however, the report, along with its accompanying road map, has yet to be released (partly a reflection of the challenging environment posed by the pandemic). The Public Expenditure and Financial Accountability report will be an important tool to help guide policy makers and development partners.

SUMMARY

Continuation of the PFM reforms that started in 2015 will be an important part of PNG's process of recovery from the COVID-19 pandemic. There is much scope to further expand revenue collection, fortify the expenditure framework, enhance financial controls, strengthen debt management, and increase transparency of public financial information. Aligned with this, it will be important for PNG to prepare strong updated medium-term strategies to guide reform and fiscal direction over the coming years. Such strategies must be government-led and carefully consider advice from external partners. Consideration of stronger and simpler fiscal rules may also be appropriate in order to facilitate adherence to medium-term fiscal frameworks.

Reference

Gaspar, V., L. Jaramillo, and P. Wingender. 2016. Tax Capacity and Growth: Is there a Tipping Point? *IMF Working Paper* No. 234. Washington, DC: International Monetary Fund. https://www.imf.org/ external/pubs/ft/wp/2016/wp16234.pdf.

The role of concessional finance in Samoa and Tonga

Lead authors: James Webb and Cara Tinio

With debt rising rapidly in Pacific island economies from the economic fallout of coronavirus disease (COVID-19), Samoa and Tonga represent two counterexamples where debt has been stable or declining. A key difference between these countries and some others in the region is the access to grant-only financing from multilateral institutions. This article explores counterfactual scenarios where Samoa and Tonga would have been required to access development finance on loan terms, and the implications for their debt position or investment portfolios in the context of the COVID-19 crisis.

BACKGROUND

In 2015, Samoa and Tonga were assessed to be at moderate risk of debt distress under the International Monetary Fund-World Bank's joint Debt Sustainability Framework for Low-Income Countries. The rating classified these countries as eligible to receive a portion of their funding from ADB and the World Bank in the form of grants, with the remainder being on concessional loan terms. After vulnerabilities to disaster risk were included in debt sustainability assessments in 2017, both countries were re-assessed to be at high risk of debt distress, causing their multilateral funding to revert to grants only.

Through accessing grant finance from their development partners, Samoa and Tonga were able to significantly increase funding received for public investments and emergency response while reducing their respective debt portfolios. Multilateral grant financing also increased dramatically following the rebasing of ADB and World Bank grant allocations (Table 3).

Table 3: ADB and World Bank project approvals, 2017-2020
($ million)

Year	Samoa		Tonga	
	ADB	World Bank	ADB	World Bank
2017	6.8	5.0	5.2	5.0
2018	10.5	55.3	16.2	69.5
2019	62.3	31.5	54.0	20.2
2020	70.0	27.9	67.2	40.4

Sources: ADB. Projects and Tenders (accessed June 2021); and World Bank. Projects & Operations (accessed June 2021).

The dramatic increase in financing in Samoa over 2018–2020 went towards projects like the $62.3 million Apia port reconstruction project (ADB 2019); cross-island road project ($40 million, ADB 2020); climate-resilient transport project ($35.8 million, World Bank 2018); and a total of $71.2 million in ADB and World Bank program-based grants for policy reforms, disaster financing, and COVID-19 support. Over the same time period in Tonga, the increase contributed to projects like those to upgrade Nuku'alofa port ($45 million, ADB 2020); improve urban facilities ($18.3 million, ADB 2019); expand transport infrastructure ($26 million, World Bank 2018); strengthen resilience to climate change and support skills and employment ($18.5 million, World Bank 2018); and support renewable energy ($12.2 million, ADB 2019); as well as a total of $100.5 million in ADB and World Bank program-based grants for policy reforms, disaster financing, and COVID-19 support.

With development finance provided on grant terms from 2018 onwards, the debt trajectories for these countries differ markedly from other Pacific nations, which can only access loans from multilateral development banks (Figure 15). Both governments also refrained from borrowing non-concessional loans from other creditors.

Figure 15: Total Public Debt in Selected Pacific Economies
% of GDP

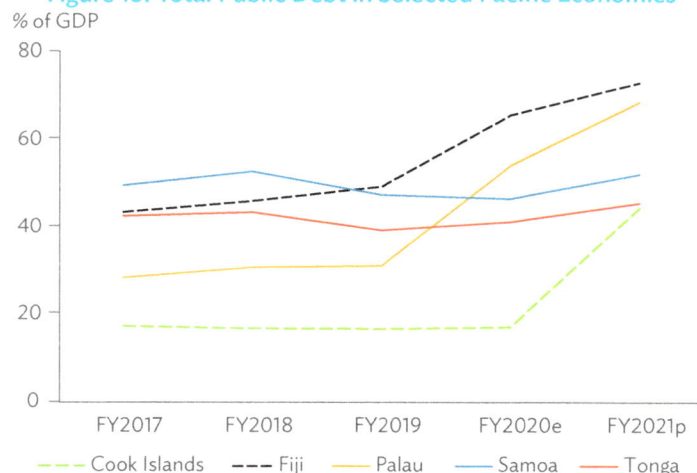

e = estimate, FY = fiscal year, GDP = gross domestic product, p = projection.
Note: Fiscal years end on 30 June of that year in the Cook Islands, Samoa, and Tonga; 31 July in Fiji; and 30 September in Palau.
Source: ADB estimates based on the Asian Development Outlook database (accessed 30 June 2021) and Government of Fiji budget releases.

Fiji and Palau both had increasing debt profiles from 2017 to 2019 because of a combination of bilateral, multilateral, and (in Fiji's case) direct sourcing of debt financing, while the Cook Islands maintained low levels of debt relative to their peers. With the COVID-19-induced economic crisis in 2020, the debt of these tourism-exposed economies rose to well above pre-crisis levels. Between FY2019 and FY2021, debt is estimated to be 27.6% of gross domestic product (GDP) higher in the Cook Islands, 23.6% of GDP higher in Fiji, and 37.4% of GDP higher in Palau. In comparison, over the same period, debt is estimated to be only 4.7% of GDP higher in Samoa and 6.2% higher in Tonga. While both economies are less exposed to the collapse in tourism than the three comparators, the lower debt pressure during the COVID-19 crisis has occurred at a time of significant fiscal stimulus and decline in domestic revenues in both Samoa and Tonga.

The comparison to other Pacific economies raises the possibility of a counterfactual scenario where grant-only financing was not offered from multilateral institutions in 2017. While a hypothetical shift to concessional or non-concessional lending may have reduced the total finance available, the reclassification of Samoa and Tonga is recent enough to speculate on what their respective debt trajectories may have been during the COVID-19 crisis.

METHODOLOGY AND ASSUMPTIONS

This exercise looks at ADB- and World Bank-funded projects and budget support from 2018 onwards, after the shift to grant-only financing terms at both institutions. The hypothetical scenarios assume that disaster risk was not considered during the International Monetary Fund assessment of debt sustainability, and there were no small-state exemptions for grant-only finance. In the simulation, these expenditures are instead funded through the "mixed finance" (about half of the funding came via loans and half funded by grants) available to Samoa and Tonga prior to 2018 or are funded completely by loans. Estimates are then made of what these countries' debt-to-GDP ratios could have looked like under these scenarios, with particular focus on the recent COVID-19 crisis period.

The "full loan terms" scenario recognizes the associated debt on a disbursement timeline of up to 5 years based on the type of project or program, or immediately on approval in the case of budget support. Contingent disaster financing arrangements for disaster response (like the ADB Pacific Disaster Resilience Program) are fully recognized upon disbursement. It is also assumed that the change from grant to loan financing had no impact on overall development spending. However, in practice, this would have had implications on the phasing of loan-funded projects and on cost-benefit assessments by both the loan recipients and lending institutions. This scenario would present the most conservative picture by reporting the largest possible counterfactual increases in debt during FY2018–FY2020. These counterfactual loans are assumed to still be in their respective grace periods, consistent with the lending policies of the multilateral institutions, and thus there would be no principal repayments between 2018 and 2021.

The "mixed finance" scenario makes similar assumptions, but instead finances development spending through grants for about half of the total loan amount assumed in the "full loan terms" scenario. This treatment is also applied to the regional financing pools used for various projects, following the treatment of eligible ADB group A mixed-finance countries.

These two scenarios were then compared with the baseline (grant-only terms) based on official data. In the case of Samoa, for which quarterly data were used, the external debt stock for a given quarter (baseline or otherwise) was compared with the sum of GDP for the past 4 quarters. US dollar amounts were converted to local currency using official period-average exchange rates prevailing at the time of project approval to facilitate comparison with the baseline scenario. The figures for Tonga are similar but were calculated for each fiscal year rather than quarterly.

RESULTS

Under the baseline scenario, Samoa's external debt declines from a peak of 52.8% at the end of June 2018 to 46.3% in December 2019, before climbing again to 49.2% in December 2020 (Figure 16). Under the full-loan counterfactual scenario, debt remains around 52.0% of GDP from June 2018 to December 2019 before rising to 56.0% in March 2020, just prior to the closure of the international border because of COVID-19. In the succeeding quarters, COVID-19 support in the form of loans, as well as the project approval for the cross-island road, would have pushed up debt to 65.4% of GDP by the end of 2020. The gap in debt-to-GDP under the baseline and counterfactual scenarios averaged 6.1% of GDP during June 2018–December 2020, and 16.2% of GDP in the last quarter of the period—a significant difference.

The mixed-finance scenario is less dramatic but still a significant departure from the baseline, with debt rising to 52.3% of GDP in the March quarter of 2020 before increasing to 57.3% of GDP by the end of the year—an 8.1 percentage point increase from the baseline.

From the equivalent of 47.9% of GDP in FY2016, public debt in Tonga under the baseline scenario falls to 43.5% in FY2018 and declines to 41.2% of GDP by FY2020 (Figure 17). But under the loan-only scenario, debt rises dramatically to 52.6% of GDP in FY2019 and then to 71.8% of GDP in FY2020. The gap between the scenarios appears more dramatic than that observed in Samoa, averaging 16.1% of GDP in FY2018–FY2020, and 30.6% of GDP by the end of FY2020.

The mixed-finance scenario follows a similar trend, with debt steadily increasing to 56.5% of GDP by the end of FY2020—a difference of 15.3 percentage points from the baseline.

Figure 16: Samoa External Debt Comparative Scenarios

COVID-19 = coronavirus disease, GDP = gross domestic product.
Source: ADB estimates based on Samoa Bureau of Statistics government finance statistics, World Bank project data, and ADB project data.

Figure 17: Tonga External Debt Comparative Scenarios

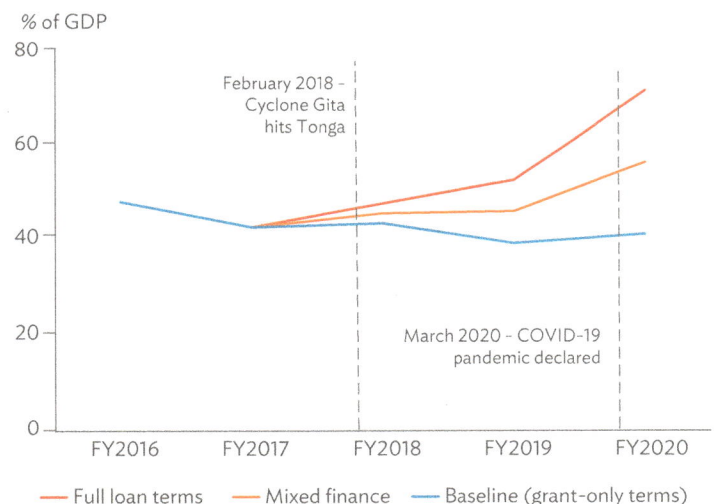

COVID-19 = coronavirus disease, FY = fiscal year, GDP = gross domestic product.
Note: The fiscal year ends 30 June of that year.
Source: ADB estimates based on National Reserve Bank of Tonga Quarterly Bulletin, World Bank project data, and ADB project data.

DISCUSSION AND CONCLUSION

In both countries, the separation among scenarios is dramatic despite only considering a 2–3-year period (though it must also be noted that this coincides with the COVID-19 pandemic, as well as the aftermath of cyclones Gita and Harold in Tonga). Considering the size of ADB and the World Bank's ongoing programs in these countries, Samoa and Tonga would likely face questions around debt sustainability post–COVID-19 pandemic if not for their reclassification to grant-only financing. Mixed finance, like what both countries could access prior to reclassification, would have alleviated these concerns somewhat by keeping the debt-to-GDP ratio below 60% by the end of FY2020. However, the pipeline of projects from multilateral institutions would have been undoubtedly less ambitious going forward given likely debt concerns. Even if the development impact had been considered appropriate for debt finance, these revisions to the forward programs may have included infrastructure projects currently being considered—for example, a cross-lagoon bridge in Tonga and the Alaoa Dam project in Samoa—because of these projects' impact on the debt profile. This is particularly true for Tonga considering that the baseline already includes a dramatic increase in debt servicing in FY2024, which would be around the same time that the concessional loans in either counterfactual scenario would be coming off their grace periods and require principal payments to commence.

The scenarios presented here are highly stylized and would have been unlikely to have materialized had reclassification not occurred. Experience in other countries in the region suggests that public investment financed through debt would lead to lower public investment overall, so the overall project portfolio would likely have been smaller than that of the grant-only baseline. Therefore, these countries would have benefited less from the infrastructure improvements that would likely have been smaller in scale, or simply not undertaken. Besides their direct impacts on power, urban conditions, and connectivity, these projects generate employment and incomes, providing some stimulus to the local economy. More importantly, reclassification has allowed the funding and implementation of climate-related projects without sacrificing government expenditure in other areas, and this was done in the face of great volatility and the largest economic crisis in the subregion's history. But if some of the investment portfolio required loan financing and would have needed to be reduced, which investments would have not gone ahead and what would the development implications have been? This is a potential area for future study that would add further depth to the analysis presented here.

Similarly, some assumptions made in this article will tend to overestimate the speed of debt accumulation in the counterfactual debt scenarios by assuming project completion within a 3- to 5-year period. Infrastructure projects in the Pacific often take many years to complete and agreed loans may not be drawn equally across the implementation period. This is particularly true of the contingent disaster financing, which is only disbursed on the realization of a disaster; this presently amounts to $10 million in ADB finance in the case of Tonga, and $20 million in the case of Samoa ($10 million from each development bank). Notably, all contingent disaster financing approved before mid-2020 has been fully drawn. Accounting for actual and estimated disbursement schedules of each project may mitigate the speed of the debt accumulation presented here but would unlikely change the final debt levels upon project completion.

Overall, while the revision in criteria on vulnerability to debt distress was based on climate, it has also effectively mitigated some of the risks posed by COVID-19 on the fiscal and debt positions of Samoa and Tonga. Access to grant-only financing has provided some breathing room even as the pandemic shrinks government resources while requiring a comprehensive response, including economic stimulus

and protection for the most vulnerable sectors. Without it, these countries would be facing an unsustainable debt burden on top of the pressing need to revitalize their economies and may have had to reduce their proposed infrastructure spending moving forward.

With relatively low and declining debt burdens, if Samoa and Tonga continue to avoid non-concessional financing sources, they appear unlikely to carry the fiscal drag or debt sustainability concerns of certain neighboring countries into the economic recovery from COVID-19. At the same time, both countries will continue to benefit from multilateral investments in climate adaptation infrastructure that will further enhance resilience going forward. This will allow for greater flexibility to manage their existing debt portfolio, guarantees, and investment needs, particularly in Tonga, where debt servicing will be challenging from 2024 onwards.

With the economic impacts from COVID-19 still impacting Fiji, and the Cook Islands' recovery being susceptible to a potentially rapid reversal if quarantine-free travel closes, the lessons from Samoa and Tonga show that efforts to mitigate climate and disaster risk through access to concessional finance can also mitigate other sources of economic risk for small island economies.

References

International Monetary Fund. *Samoa: Staff Report for the Article IV Consultation—Debt Sustainability Analysis.* Washington, DC (7 years: 2015, 2017–2021).

International Monetary Fund. *Tonga: Staff Report for the Article IV Consultation—Debt Sustainability Analysis.* Washington, DC (2 years: 2017, 2020).

J. Saito. 2018. The revised low-income country debt sustainability framework and the Pacific. *Pacific Economic Monitor.* December.

Level up: raising the quality of labor in Solomon Islands

Lead authors: Prince Cruz and Dalcy Ilala

The economy of Solomon Islands has started to recover in 2021 after it contracted by about 4.5% in 2020. Growth is seen to be 1.0% this year before accelerating in 2022 as trade and travel restrictions continue to be lifted. The government has responded to the challenges of the coronavirus disease (COVID-19) pandemic impact by reorienting its 2019 policy statement and strategy into a "2020 policy redirection."

The redirection policy aims to keep the economy afloat and accelerate recovery by protecting vulnerable people, mitigating the damage the pandemic has inflicted on the economy, and bolstering economic resilience. A key component of the redirection policy is Strategy 6 which aims to "Increase employment and labor mobility opportunities in rural areas and improve the livelihoods of all Solomon Islanders."[1] The policy focuses on investments that develop technical and industry-appropriate skills (rather than traditional education that focuses more on "academic or institutional knowledge"). It also prioritizes a multitier scholarship program inclusive of skill-based performance. The government also aims to develop a skill-based strategy to end the notion of "student dropout."

Improving the quality of labor in Solomon Islands through better education, training, and skills upgrading will not only help the economy get back to pre-crisis levels faster, but also minimize the effects of similar crises in the future. They would also allow more Solomon Islanders to benefit from expanding employment opportunities, such as Australia's Pacific Labour Scheme.

THE STATE OF THE LABOR MARKET

The Central Bank of Solomon Islands reported that the number of employed fell 8.7% in 2020 based on Solomon Islands National Provident Fund contributors. This likely reflects the impact of COVID-19 on formal employment. The impact on the informal sector would be more difficult to assess because of lack of data, but would likely be substantial because of the lack of safety nets.

Data from the 2015 Demographic and Health Survey shed light on several aspects of the labor market.[2] More than 50% of women but only 25% of men were not employed in the past 12 months preceding the survey (Table 4).[3] Further, only 37% of women but

70% of men were employed at the time of the survey. The disparity in employment between men and women was similar in urban and rural areas.

A link between employment and education can also be inferred from the survey. The percentage of men and women employed was highest among those with education beyond the secondary level. The disparity in employment outcome based on education is more distinct for women: 66% of women with more than secondary education were currently employed, against about 35% for those with less education. For men, more than 80% of those with more than secondary education were employed. Interestingly, almost 78% of men with no education were employed, higher than those with primary (71%) or secondary education (66%).

In terms of location, the percentage of men of and women employed was lower in the three biggest provinces (Malaita, Western, and Guadalcanal) and the capital city, Honiara, compared to other provinces. The percentage of men not employed in the past 12 months was highest in Honiara and its surrounding province Guadalcanal. For women, more than 50% in Honiara and the three biggest provinces were not employed in the past 12 months, significantly higher than the 31% in other provinces.

While agriculture accounts for about one-third of the economy, it employed more than half (54%) of men and 41% of women workers in 2015 (Figure 18). After agriculture-related work, men engaged in skilled manual labor while women worked in sales and services. Only 12% of men and 15% of women worked as professionals.

Table 4: Employment Status of Men and Women in Solomon Islands, 2015
(% of adults aged 15–49)

	Men			Women		
	Employed in Past 12 Months		Not Employed in Past 12 Months	Employed in Past 12 Months		Not Employed in Past 12 Months
	Currently Employed	Not Currently Employed		Currently Employed	Not Currently Employed	
All	70.0	5.4	24.5	37.1	9.6	53.3
Location						
Urban	62.7	4.9	32.2	40.9	3.3	55.6
Rural	72.3	5.6	22.0	35.9	11.4	52.6
Province/city						
Honiara	59.5	3.7	36.7	36.3	1.7	61.9
Guadalcanal	59.5	6.5	34.0	43.4	5.5	51.0
Malaita	74.0	1.8	24.2	24.7	7.1	68.1
Western	70.4	11.3	18.3	31.9	5.8	62.0
Other provinces	80.0	5.7	13.9	47.8	20.9	31.3
Education						
No education	77.7	4.2	18.1	31.6	11.8	56.5
Primary	70.9	6.0	22.9	35.8	11.3	52.8
Secondary	65.8	5.5	28.6	35.1	7.6	57.2
More than secondary	82.4	3.1	14.5	66.4	6.2	27.4

Source: Solomon Islands 2015 Demographic and Health Survey.

Figure 18: Occupation of Employed Workers in Solomon Islands, 2015

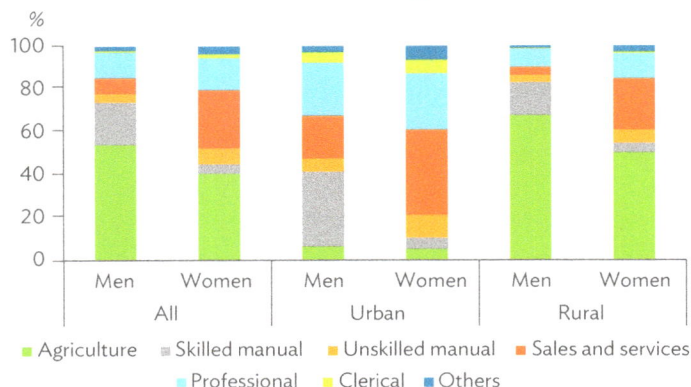

Note: Workers aged 15–49 employed in the 12 months preceding the survey.
Source: Solomon Islands 2015 Demographic and Health Survey.

For women employed in agriculture, 80% were not paid whereas only 27% were unpaid in non-agricultural jobs. These unpaid workers were mostly employed by family members or self-employed. Cash payment was provided to 13% of agricultural workers and 60% of non-agricultural workers. Unfortunately, similar data for men were not provided in the survey.

Figure 19: Mode of Payment for Women Workers in Solomon Islands, 2015

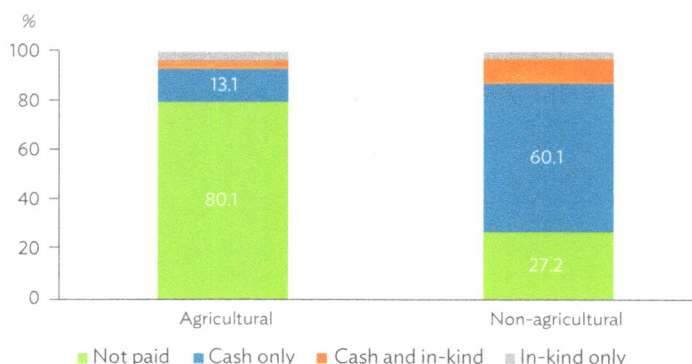

Note: Workers aged 15–49 employed in the 12 months preceding the survey.
Source: Solomon Islands 2015 Demographic and Health Survey.

The survey also showed the literacy rate at 89% for men and 82% for women in 2015, lower than the 91% for men and 88% for women reported in the 2009 Census. There was a disparity between urban and rural areas with literacy rates in rural areas at 80% for women (against 91% in urban) and 88% for men (95% urban) (Figure 20). In Western province, the literacy rate of women (95%) was slightly higher than men (92%). In Malaita, the gap between literacy rates of men and women was the highest at more than 10 percentage points (84% for men and 71% for women). The gap in literacy between men and women was almost 20 percentage points for those belonging in the poorest quintile (65% for women versus 83% for men) while it is not much for those in the richest quintile (93% of women and 95% for men).

Figure 20: Literacy Rate in Solomon Islands, 2015

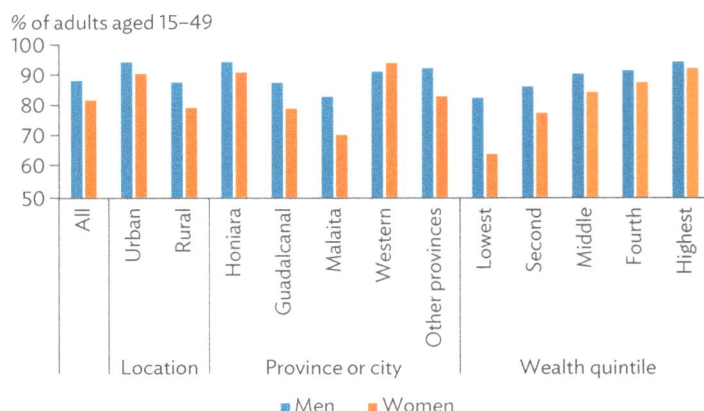

Source: Solomon Islands 2015 Demographic and Health Survey.

LABOR MOBILITY PROGRAMS

The redirection policy puts great emphasis on promotion and facilitation of programs that support the transfer and exchange of appropriate skills and knowledge. The measures to support this particular redirection policy included (i) supporting labor mobility programs with Australia and New Zealand, and (ii) encouraging collaboration between local and foreign investors.

The Government of Australia addressed the pandemic's impact in the Pacific by building on its existing Pacific foreign policy priorities. In August 2020, it recommended recruitment under the Pacific Labour Scheme and the Seasonal Workers Programme, which are designed to alleviate persistent workforce shortages in critical sectors of the Australian economy. COVID-19 outbreaks in Papua New Guinea and Fiji have increased opportunities for Solomon Island workers and, between November 2020 and May 2021, more than 1,000 workers were employed in Australia.[4] Solomon Islands is currently ranked in the top three countries with the highest number of seasonal workers in Australia. The projected target is 2,000 Solomon Islands workers for 2021.

To take advantage of the labor mobility program and to increase Solomon Islands workers' chances of being selected for the labor mobility scheme, the Solomon Islands Labour Mobility Strategy proposed training interventions. The Australia Pacific Training Coalition (APTC) is partnering with the Pacific Labour Facility in Solomon Islands to train Pacific workers to meet workforce demands by Australian employers under the scheme. In June 2021, APTC delivered training on work, health, and safety measures to 10 Solomon Islands workers who will work in the Australian construction industry.[5]

CHALLENGES AHEAD

The government is preparing for recovery through a vaccination drive against COVID-19. Despite having one of the earliest rollouts in March 2021, only 3.0% of the population had received at least one dose as of 20 July (page 33). Solomon Islands has received 24,000 doses from COVAX, 50,000 doses from the People's Republic of China, and 28,800 doses from New Zealand/COVAX (enough to fully vaccinate about 7.1% of the population). With the low take-up from priority groups (health care workers, older people, and persons with comorbidities), the government opened vaccination to all adults aged 18 and above on 22 June. There have been 20 cases of COVID-19 in Solomon Islands, all brought in by returning residents and expatriates.

The tight fiscal situation would require the government to carefully balance the needs of different sectors of society. The need for improving education and skills is massive, especially in rural areas. The 2021 budget seeks to cut the deficit from SI\$622 million (equivalent to 5.1% of GDP) to SI\$338 million (2.7% of GDP). Total revenue is projected to decline by 2.7% mainly because of grants falling by 10.3%. The reduction in the deficit will largely be done through an 8.7% cut in expenditure with recurrent expenses falling by 11.9%. Several ministries, including those providing social services such as education and health, experienced reductions in allocation under the 2021 budget.

Figure 21: Budget of Various Ministries in Solomon Islands

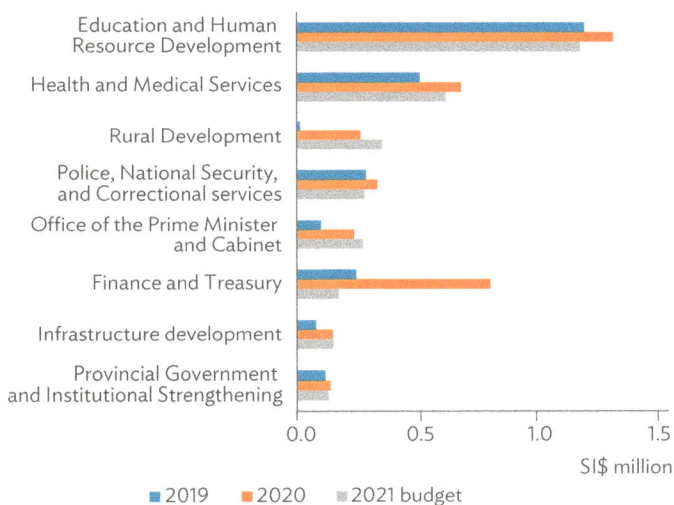

Source: Solomon Islands Ministry of Finance and Treasury budget documents.

Endnotes

[1]   Strategy 6 is aligned with Objective 1 of the National Development Strategy 2016–2035: Sustained and Inclusive Economic Growth, and Medium Term.

[2]   The survey, published online in 2020, focuses more on health aspects (such as fertility, maternal and child nutrition, and access to health services) of households with more female than male respondents (6,266 women and 3,591 men). The background information on the respondents, however, can still provide useful data on several aspects of the economy. Solomon Islands National Statistics Office. 2017. *2015 Demographic and Health Survey*. Honiara.

[3]   The figure for "not employed" is different from "unemployed." Unemployed refers to people who are not employed but currently looking for work. For those "not employed," it was not indicated in the survey if they are looking for work.

[4]   Government of Solomon Islands, Ministry of Foreign Affairs, and External Trade. 2021. *LMU sends another large group of workers to Australia*. http://www.mfaet.gov.sb/media-center/press-releases/external-trade-news/231-lmu-sends-another-large-group-of-workers-to-australia.html.

[5]   Australia Pacific Training Coalition. 2021. *Solomon Islanders receive work, health and safety training for employment in Australia's construction sector*. https://aptc.edu.au/news/news/2021/06/03/solomon-islanders-receive-work-health-and-safety-training-for-employment-in-australia-s-construction-sector.

Gearing up for recovery: COVID-19 and the private sector in Vanuatu

Lead authors: Prince Cruz and Nancy Wells

In 2020, Vanuatu's economy contracted by 8.5%, the biggest contraction since independence, mainly because of the coronavirus disease (COVID-19) pandemic. The situation was exacerbated by tropical cyclone (TC) Harold, which struck in April 2020 affecting more than 130,000 people (about 43% of the population) and damaging homes, schools, medical facilities, and crops; seriously impeding access to essential services; and compromising food security for many Ni-Vanuatu.[1] The combined economic cost of COVD-19 and TC Harold has been estimated at Vt68.1 billon (equivalent to almost 70% of gross domestic product [GDP]). These dual crises sit within the broader context of Vanuatu's long-term development challenges—distance from major markets, climate change and disaster vulnerability, and limited options for economic diversification.

Although Vanuatu has one of the most vibrant private sectors in the Pacific, it is still relatively small. A labor market survey in 2000 found that almost 70% of respondents were engaged in subsistence activities.[2] Further, whereas in other Pacific countries the public sector is commonly the biggest formal sector employer, in Vanuatu almost twice as many respondents were employed in the private sector than in the public sector (Figure 22).

The dominance of the subsistence sector was confirmed by the 2016 Mini-Census. Nationally, only 30% of the population were employed (43,571), while 35% (51,413) were producing goods with an additional 30% (43,828) as unpaid family workers (Figure 23). It was only in the two urban areas (Port Vila, the capital, and Luganville) that more than 50% were employed. In rural areas, only 20% were employed. Among the provinces, Shefa, which includes Port Vila, has the highest share of employed people.

Figure 22: Main Economic Engagement in Vanuatu, 1999–2000

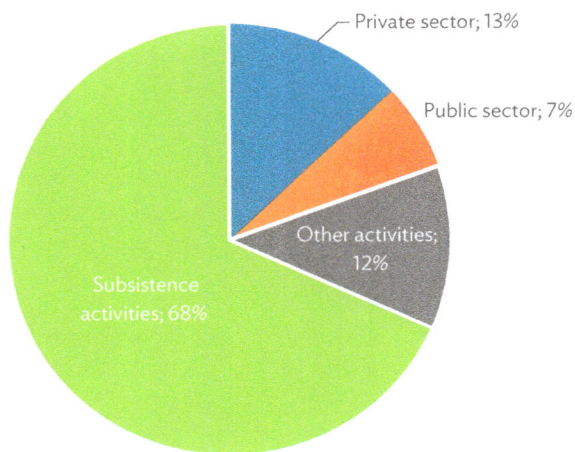

Source: United Nations Economic and Social Commission for Asia and the Pacific (UNESCAP). 2007. Improving Employment Opportunities in Pacific Island Developing Countries. *Small Island Developing States Series*, No. 1. https://www.unescap.org/sites/default/files/Impoving-employment-opportunities-in-PIDCs.pdf.

Figure 23: Main Economic Activity in Vanuatu, 2016

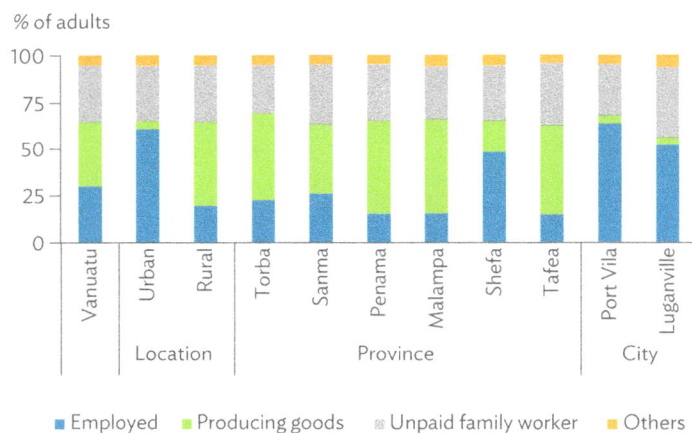

Notes: Adults aged 15 and above in private households. Others include those engaged in volunteer work and economically inactive people.
Source: Vanuatu National Statistics Office. 2016. *Post Pam Mini Census Report*, Volume 1. Port Vila.

IMPACT ON THE PRIVATE SECTOR

The effects of COVID-19 on private business were captured in the Vanuatu Economic Outlook Report, published by the Vanuatu Chamber of Commerce and Industry (VCCI) in September 2020.[3] Respondents in the survey included more than 200 businesses located all over Vanuatu and covering various sectors.[4]

On the average, respondents reported a 50% drop in revenues in August 2020 from a year earlier, with accommodation and restaurants declaring a significantly higher 79% income fall (Figure 24). Other sectors that reported a more than 50% drop in

revenue included transport, other services, and agriculture. Finance and insurance companies reported the lowest decline in revenues (11%) followed by construction (19%).

Figure 24: Change in Revenue and Workers in Vanuatu, 2020

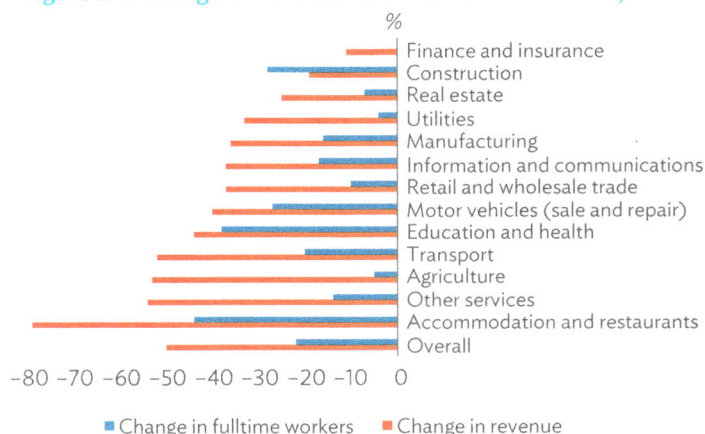

Notes:
1. Change in revenue from August 2019 (pre-pandemic period) to August 2020 is based on average change reported by respondents in each sector.
2. Change in workers based on all workers hired by the respondents in each sector.
Source: Vanuatu Chamber of Commerce and Industry. 2020. *Vanuatu Economic Outlook Report*. https://vcci.vu/vanuatu-economic-outlook-report-from-a-private-sectors-perspective/.

The number of full-time workers declined by 22% (from 3,871 to 3,028), and part-time workers by 13.7%. In terms of sectors, accommodation and restaurants and other services reported the highest reduction in fulltime employees at more than 40%, while finance and insurance reported no change in employment.

VCCI businesses have been using extraordinary measures to remain afloat—with 45% of respondents reported using personal savings in some capacity to help fund their businesses. This coping strategy is not sustainable, and without a recovery in demand, it is highly likely that several of these businesses will close, either temporarily or permanently. Further, 26% of the surveyed VCCI firms indicated that they would shut down if demand would fall further by 20%.

Many businesses tried hard to retain staff by reducing working hours or cutting other costs, but 46% of businesses said they had plans to lay off staff. The highest percentage of respondents planning redundancies was in accommodation and restaurants (68%), followed by retail and wholesale trade (59%), construction (42%), information and communication (40%), and transport (36%). Further redundancies would lead to lower aggregate demand, and other firms could follow in laying off staff.

The effects of COVID-19 on business in Vanuatu can also be gleaned from a series of surveys conducted by Pacific Trade Invest, a unit of the Pacific Islands Forum Secretariat.[5] Nine surveys—referred to as waves—were conducted in 2020 on 16 Pacific economies. More than 110 firms were surveyed in each wave. Waves 1–3 were conducted from May to June, waves 4 and 5 from July to August, waves 6 and 7 from September to October, and waves 8 and 9 from November to December. In Vanuatu, the number of respondents ranged from 7 to 20 in each wave.

In waves 1–3, 21% of respondents said they were either temporarily or permanently closed. This increased to 24% in waves 4–5 before declining to 18% in waves 6–7 and 15% in waves 8–9. When asked about the impact of COVID-19 on their business, the percentage of respondents saying that it was very negative increased from 72% in waves 1–3 to 85% in waves 8–9 (Figure 25). On the other hand, those who said the impact was positive fluctuated from 8% in waves 1–3, to 12% in waves 4–5, none in waves 6–7, and 10% in waves 8–9.

Figure 25: Impact of COVID-19 on Businesses in Vanuatu, 2020

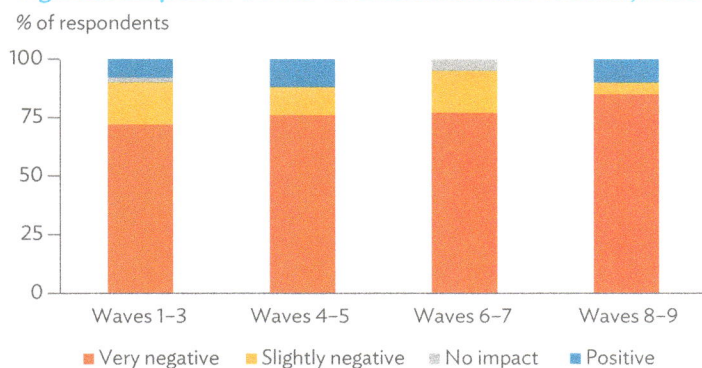

% of respondents

■ Very negative   ■ Slightly negative   ▨ No impact   ■ Positive

COVID-19 = coronavirus disease.
Source: Pacific Trade Invest. 2020. *Pacific Business Monitor 2020: Vanuatu Focus.* https://www.pacifictradeinvest.com/services/pti-pacific-business-monitor.

LOOKING AT TOURISM BUSINESSES

With international travel restricted, businesses relying on tourism were affected the most, especially those in Port Vila and Luganville, which are centers of tourism. International tourism started strong in 2020 with air arrivals in the first 2 months up by 20% year-on-year and cruise ship visitors more than doubling. The numbers dropped rapidly before the border closed on 21 March 2020, and there have not been any international visitors since. The VCCI reported in September 2020 that businesses including handicraft vendors and bus drivers whose income (70% and 40%, respectively) come from tourists have now scaled down or gone out of business. Hotels and resorts have been forced to close or reduce their operation, and this involved scaling down of their staff numbers.

The Department of Tourism conducted two surveys in 2020 to assess the impact on tourism businesses. In the first survey in April 2020, 55% of respondents said they remained fully operational (the other 45% said they had already closed). In the follow-up survey in August, only 21% said they remained fully open. The remaining respondents indicated that they were partially operational (39%), closed but intends to reopen (37%), or closed indefinitely (3%).[6]

Businesses in the tourism industry are categorized into: large (more than 25 employees), medium (6–25 employees), and small (5

or fewer employees) (Table 5). In total, they have about 11,500 employees: about a third under large firms, about half under medium-sized firms, and less than 20% under small firms.[7] Large firms include hotels and resorts. Medium-sized firms include motels, tour operators, rental vehicles (including planes and helicopters), souvenir shops, and various food establishments. Small firms include smaller accommodations (such as guest houses and home stays), transport (e.g., buses, taxis, and boats), and activities and tour agencies.

Table 5: Vanuatu Tourism Businesses

Category	Large 25+ Employees	Medium 6–25 Employees	Small 1–5 Employees
Number of firms (% of total)	91 (6%)	645 (39%)	920 (55%)
Number of employees (% of total)	3,640 (32%)	5,616 (49%)	2,237 (19%)

Source: Government of Vanuatu Department of Tourism 2021.

About 89% of large tourism businesses indicated that they find it hard or very hard to recruit Ni-Vanuatu workers with required skills. To bridge the skills gap, they employ foreigners and provide internal training. These businesses are typically foreign-owned.

Medium-sized business also encounter difficulties in hiring workers with the required skills (based on 85% of respondents). These owners typically have high involvement in business operations. Their staff are usually "multi-skilled" (i.e., performs different functions) and hired through family and community networks. The businesses are not confident in running their own internal training but provide nonformal learning ways for training staff.

Small tourism businesses are mostly owned by Ni-Vanuatu individuals or families and staffed by family members. Most owners and employees do not have formal qualifications, and they have the lowest confidence in terms of providing own training. They have strong demand for on-the-job training and training done in vernacular language.

DOING BUSINESS IN VANUATU

Vanuatu ranked 107 out of 190 economies in the 2020 World Bank Doing Business report (Figure 26).[8] It was only in three categories that it ranked among the top 50%: getting credit, paying taxes, and registering property.

Vanuatu's worst rank was in terms of dealing with construction permits, a particular problem for tourism businesses in Vanuatu, which is highly susceptible to natural hazards such as cyclones. The number of procedures and days for dealing with construction permit in Vanuatu is similar to its neighbors and the average for East Asia and the Pacific (Table 6). It was in terms of the cost and building quality control wherein Vanuatu lagged behind.

The pandemic further raised the cost of trading across borders. The VCCI reported in 2020 that sea freight costs have risen by 30%, and those of air freight by 150%–300%. International trade has become riskier and more difficult because of the time lag to import or export, as well as uncertainty about whether shipments would actually happen. Some local firms have had to wait for more than 3 months to receive spare parts to repair machinery.

Figure 26: Ease of Doing Business in Vanuatu, 2020

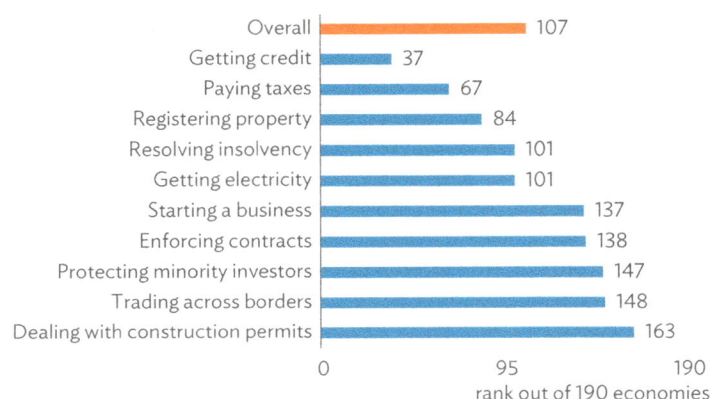

Source: World Bank. 2020. *Doing Business 2020: Economy Profile Vanuatu.* Washington, DC.

Table 6: Dealing with Construction Permits in Vanuatu and Other Economies, 2020

	Vanuatu	Fiji	Solomon Islands	East Asia and the Pacific
Rank (out of 190 economies)	163	102	172	84
Procedures	15.0	15.0	14.0	14.8
Number of days	123.0	141.0	92.0	132.3
Cost (% of warehouse value)	9.4	0.5	19.7	3.2
Building quality control index (0–15)	5.0	7.0	8.0	9.4

Source: World Bank. 2020. *Doing Business 2020: Region Profile East Asia and the Pacific.* Washington, DC.

A CONDUCIVE ENVIRONMENT FOR THE PRIVATE SECTOR?

A difficult business environment for the private sector in Vanuatu has been compounded by the effects of TC Harold and the COVID-19 pandemic, and the situation remains uncertain as countries continue to impose lockdowns in response to different variants of the virus. There is much uncertainty as to when borders will reopen to allow for the return of tourists. It is important that the government foster an environment that is conducive to the preservation and recovery of the private sector. Addressing the skill needs of the tourism sector will be a key element of any program.

In recognition of this, the government and the tourism industry stakeholders developed the Vanuatu Tourism Human Resource Development Strategy 2021–2030, which identified 13 objectives with corresponding implementing approaches and performance indicators. The objectives include increases in the quantity and quality of training, better accreditation processes, improved learning resources, and better events management.

In response to the COVID-19 pandemic in general, the government formulated the Vanuatu Sustainable Tourism Strategy 2021–2025.[9] It focuses on transition to a more resilient economy that is less dependent on the tourism industry and aims to ensure that the undesirable aspects of the tourism industry do not return. The strategy puts forward targets and programs that will ensure that the economy is better diversified to support more local industries and livelihoods. One of the four themes in the strategy focuses on diversification through agritourism. This is in collaboration with Pacific Agribusiness Research for Development Initiative 2, a theme to promote activities to regenerate Vanuatu's assets, including its culture, customs, environment, communities, and traditional economy. Further, the strategy aims to create more meaningful jobs and, at the same time, deal with the bottlenecks in the supply chains for tourism to ensure local value-added products.

The 2021 budget lists "enhanced business opportunities and investment environment" as its first of seven priority outcomes.[10] Other priority outcomes such as (number 2) improved resilient infrastructure and (number 3) improved education quality and accessibility would also boost the private sector. Under the target outcomes, the government indicated that it would increase support to local entrepreneurships and cooperative movement. Access to financial capital and financial literacy would also be improved. Under education, the government aims to improve "opportunities for employability and entrepreneurial skills development – through technical and vocational skills training and increased support for out of school youth."

If accomplished, the list of target outcomes under the 2021 budget would significantly boost the private sector and improve business environment. However, this could prove to be challenging as the government faces tightening fiscal space. From an average of 4.5% of GDP in 2018–2019, the fiscal surplus dropped to 0.4% of GDP in 2020.

In May 2021, the government announced details of the Second Policy Stimulus package to support businesses, especially small and medium-sized enterprises.[11] The schemes under the second stimulus include:

- Vt600 million for Small Business Grants to support monthly cash flow of businesses with an annual turnover of less than Vt 4 million until the end of 2021;

- Vt560 million for a Wage Subsidy Scheme to support businesses that are value-added tax-registered and distressed with their staffing costs until the end of 2021; and

- Vt900 million for a Special COVID-19 Banking Facility to stabilize businesses' balance sheets, which has the potential to run for as long as 5 years. The facility will support the five major commercial banks to provide a guarantee for additional credit to clients that have faced hardship during the pandemic.

The hope is that the second stimulus package worth Vt2.1 billion (2.0% of GDP), will support part of the private sector. The second stimulus is on top of Vt5.1 billion stimulus approved in 2020. Despite the stimulus packages, a private sector-led recovery would be difficult as borders remain closed.

Endnotes

1   Government of Vanuatu. 2020. *Post-Disaster Needs Assessment TC Harold & COVID-19*. Volumes A and B. Port Vila.

2   United Nations Economic and Social Commission for Asia and the Pacific (UNESCAP). 2007. Improving Employment Opportunities in Pacific Island Developing Countries. *Small Island Developing States Series*, No. 1. https://www.unescap.org/sites/default/files/Impoving-employment-opportunities-in-PIDCs.pdf.

3   Vanuatu Chamber of Commerce and Industry. 2020. *Vanuatu Economic Outlook Report*. https://vcci.vu/vanuatu-economic-outlook-report-from-a-private-sectors-perspective/.

4   About 27% of the respondents belong to the accommodation and restaurants sector, 19% from "other services," 14% from retail and wholesale trade, 13% from manufacturing, 7% from transport, 6% from construction, 3% from finance and insurance, 3% from information and communication, 3% from education and health, 2% from real estate, 1% from agriculture, and 1% from utilities. The report indicated there were 203 respondents, but the breakdown by sector only adds up to 188. Further, no respondents were reported under motor vehicle (sales and repair) but there are corresponding answers under that sector. By province, 85% of respondents were from Shefa (which includes Port Vila), 12% from Sanma (which includes Luganville), and the rest (3%) from Tafea and Malampa.

5   Pacific Trade Invest. 2020. *Pacific Business Monitor 2020: Vanuatu Focus.* Pacific Islands Forum Secretariat. https://www.pacifictradeinvest.com/services/pti-pacific-business-monitor.

6   Government of Vanuatu Department of Tourism. 2020. *Vanuatu National Tourism Impact Survey 2020*. https://tourism.gov.vu/images/DoT-Documents/Presentations/Vanuatu_national_Tourism_Business_Impact_survey-2020.pdf.

7   Government of Vanuatu Department of Tourism. 2021. *Vanuatu Tourism Human Resource Development Strategy 2021–2030*. https://tourism.gov.vu/images/DoT-Documents/Plans/VANUATU_TOURISM_HUMAN_RESOURCES_DEVELOPMENT_STRATEGY_2021__2030.pdf.

8   World Bank. *Doing Business 2020: Economy Profile Vanuatu*. Washington, DC. https://www.doingbusiness.org/content/dam/doingBusiness/country/v/vanuatu/VUT.pdf.

9   Government of Vanuatu Department of Tourism. 2021. *Vanuatu Sustainable Tourism Strategy 2021–2025*. https://tourism.gov.vu/images/DoT-Documents/Plans/Vanuatu_Sustainable_Tourism_Strategy_LR.pdf.

10   Government of Vanuatu Department of Finance and Treasury. 2020. *2021 Budget Book*. Volumes 1 and 2. https://doft.gov.vu/images/2021/Budget/Book/2021_Budget_Book_Volume_1__2_English.pdf.

11   Government of Vanuatu, Department of Finance and Treasury. 2021. *Second Policy Stimulus Press Release No. 2 of 2021*. https://doft.gov.vu/images/2021/covid-19/Second_Press_Release.pdf.

POLICY BRIEFS

Jab security: Broadening COVID-19 vaccination coverage in the Pacific

The majority of Pacific countries have prevented community transmission of coronavirus disease (COVID-19) by closing their borders and setting up quarantine systems. Preemptive trade and travel restrictions to keep out the virus have had significant negative economic impacts across the subregion, particularly on countries reliant on tourism for growth. Pacific countries have joined the global drive to vaccinate their populations against COVID-19, which is key to enable the reopening of borders and resumption of economic activity. Progress in immunization coverage of the first dose, however, has been uneven across the subregion. This policy brief presents the COVID-19 situation and vaccine coverage in the Pacific and examines the constraints to broadening vaccination across the subregion.

COVID-19 IN THE PACIFIC

Tale of the tape: the pandemic in numbers. The path of the pandemic in the Pacific has taken a turn for the worse for the subregion's most populous countries. Since the first quarter of this year, total confirmed cases of COVID-19 have increased sharply in Papua New Guinea (PNG) and Fiji. The subregion's largest country in terms of population and economic size, PNG saw its first confirmed case in March 2020. The number of cases remained low throughout 2020 but a rapid rise in 2021 has placed enormous strain on the country's health system with the total caseload at over 17,000 and close to 200 reported COVID-19 deaths as of 7 July.

Meanwhile, Fiji had largely managed to contain the spread of the virus until widespread community transmission started in April this year involving the highly contagious Delta variant.[1] In a bid to contain further spread of the disease, lockdowns were imposed in containment areas linked to various case clusters, though authorities have ruled out a nationwide lockdown. As of 15 July, the country's total caseload stands at 12,666 cases with 69 related deaths. While the surge in PNG seems to have abated, new cases continue to rise in Fiji and infections with no clear links to existing clusters are an increasing cause of concern (Figure 1). The World Health Organization (WHO) has classified Fiji's Central Division as experiencing large-scale community transmission, while the Western Division is experiencing localized community transmission.

For the rest of the subregion, a few countries have recorded cases largely from repatriated citizens but have remained free of local community transmission. As the experience of Fiji shows, however, the situation can change rapidly once the virus bypasses border control measures and enters the local community. The challenge is compounded by the emergence of even more transmissible COVID-19 variants and their potential for immunological escape vis-a-vis existing vaccines.

Figure 1: Number of Reported Cases in Papua New Guinea and Fiji
(cumulative total)

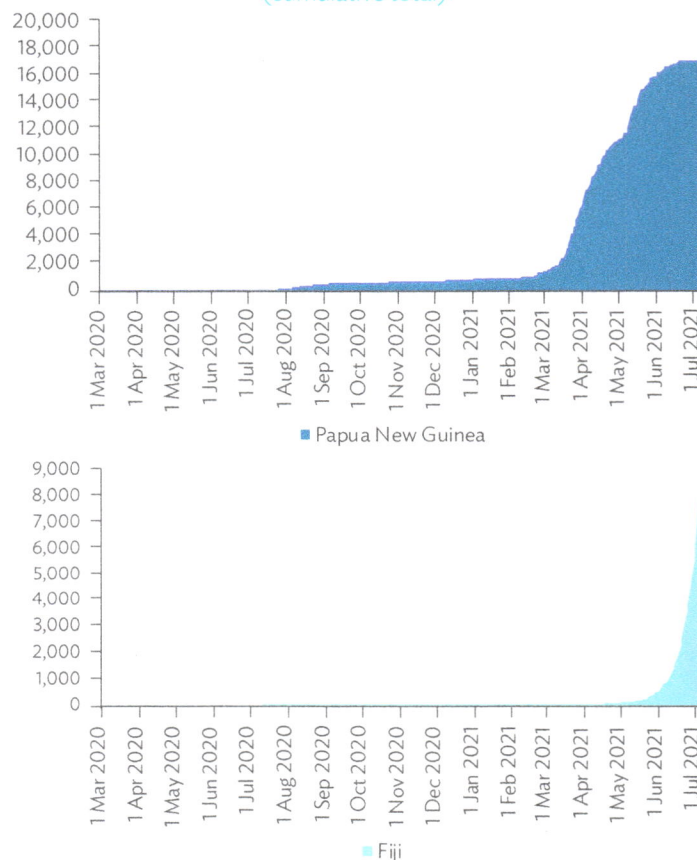

■ Papua New Guinea

■ Fiji

Note: Data as of 7 July 2021.
Source: M. Roser, H. Ritchie, E. Ortiz-Ospina, and J. Hasell. 2020. *Coronavirus Pandemic (COVID-19)*. https://ourworldindata.org/coronavirus (accessed 9 July 2021).

Minding the gap between the jabs and the jab-nots. All ADB developing member countries (DMCs) in the Pacific have introduced one or more COVID-19 vaccines, with varying success. The North Pacific economies of the Federated States of Micronesia (FSM), the Marshall Islands, and Palau were among the earliest to begin inoculating their populations in January 2021, using United States (US)-procured vaccines under the Operation Warp Speed of the Government of the US. While a relatively rapid rollout has led to high vaccination coverage in Palau, the FSM has faced logistics challenges in getting vaccines to the outer islands.

While the North Pacific economies have benefited from support from the US, the Cook Islands and Niue accessed vaccines through

New Zealand and achieved high coverage relatively soon after introduction. Nauru was able to administer the first dose to its entire adult population within 1 month after receiving doses from Australia, through the COVID-19 Vaccines Global Access (COVAX) facility and additional supplies from the government of India.

In terms of population coverage, Palau has issued the first dose to about 80% of its total population, followed by Nauru (70%), and the Cook Islands (62%) (Figure 2). Palau also leads in terms of the share of its population that has been fully vaccinated at 78%, followed by Nauru (64%), and the Cook Islands (55%). Currently, data are scarce on the number of the fully vaccinated for many other countries that either started their vaccination rollouts later (after the first quarter of 2021) or are still trying to secure sufficient supplies.

Figure 2: Vaccination Coverage
(% of total population)

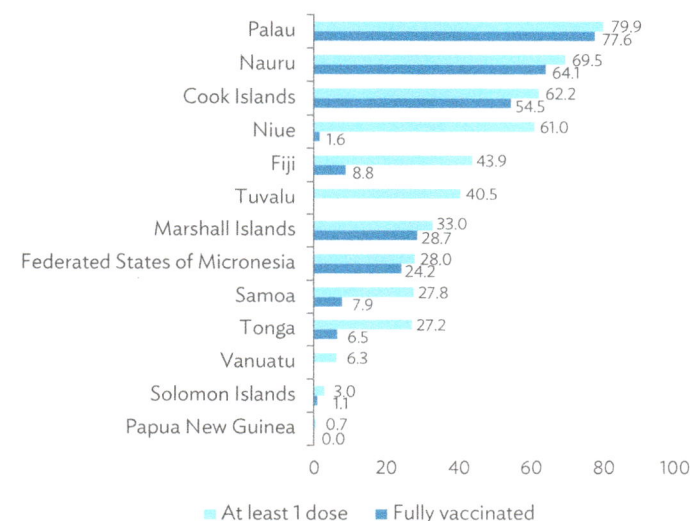

Notes: Currently, data are not publicly available for Kiribati. Data as of 20 July 2021. Sources: M. Roser, H. Ritchie, E. Ortiz-Ospina, and J. Hasell. 2020. *Coronavirus Pandemic (COVID-19)*. https://ourworldindata.org/coronavirus (accessed 23 July 2021); Pacific Data Hub. 2020. *COVID-19 vaccination.* https://pacificdata.org (accessed 23 July 2021); and authors' calculations.

As countries achieve their target vaccine coverage, they will progressively start to open to international travelers. Palau and the Cook Islands' initial efforts to open their borders with major bilateral partners highlight the fragility of travel bubbles and the importance of vaccination as a prerequisite for the safe easing of restrictions. In the same vein, Samoa announced that high vaccination coverage will be a prerequisite for reopening its borders and that it is discussing with New Zealand and Australia how to secure additional vaccines on top of their allocation from the COVAX facility.

While small, single-island states like Nauru and Niue have vaccinated their entire adult populations, Pacific DMCs still face various challenges to their respective vaccine rollouts. Countries

with larger and more dispersed populations, as well as those with a higher proportion of children (for which most COVID-19 vaccines are currently not recommended), will find it more difficult to move towards universal vaccine coverage. Based on available data as of 20 July, only about 6% of the total population in Pacific DMCs had received at least one COVID-19 vaccine dose and less than 2% had been fully vaccinated (Table 1).

Table 1: Vaccine Coverage in ADB's Pacific Developing Member Countries

Country	First Dose	Second Dose	Target Population*	Total Population	Start of Vaccinations
Cook Islands	10,931	9,578	15,000	17,564	May
Fiji	393,095	78,624	650,000	896,444	March
Kiribati	...	...	...	119,446	May
Marshall Islands	19,536	16,977	29,000	59,194	January
Federated States of Micronesia	32,215	27,879	58,699	115,021	January
Nauru	7,529	6,949	6,812	10,834	April
Niue	1,184	32	1,115	1,940	June
Palau	14,464	14,038	14,400	18,094	January
Papua New Guinea	63,376	2975	...	8,947,027	March
Samoa	55,061	15,650	120,000	198,410	April
Solomon Islands	20,538	7,282	450,000	686,878	March
Tonga	28,729	6,906	70,000	105,697	April
Tuvalu	4,772	...	6,400	11,792	April
Vanuatu	19,332	...	...	307,150	June
Total (Pacific subregion)	670,762	186,890			
% of total population	5.8	1.6			

* = adult population, ... = data not available, ADB = Asian Development Bank.
Notes:
1. Data as of 20 July 2021.
2. Population numbers are estimates where official data is unavailable.
3. Target population is based on approximation of adults aged 18 and above.
Sources: M. Roser, H. Ritchie, E. Ortiz-Ospina, and J. Hasell. 2020. *Coronavirus Pandemic* (COVID-19). https://ourworldindata.org/coronavirus (accessed 23 July 2021); Pacific Data Hub. 2020.. COVID-19 vaccination. Retrieved from: https://pacificdata.org (accessed 23 July 2021); authors' calculations; various news sources.

Many countries are pushing to vaccinate their populations with a view towards easing border restrictions, especially for those with major economic activities dependent on open borders—such as tourism for Palau and the Cook Islands, and foreign fishing activities for the FSM and the Marshall Islands. Unsurprisingly, therefore, countries that are expected to suffer slower or more negative growth this year relative to 2019 are also the ones leading the race to vaccinate their populations (Figure 3). This is because of the anticipation of steep losses in economic activity due to prolonged public health measures and mobility restrictions.

Unfortunately, vaccination coverage remains uneven and is skewed in favor of higher-income countries (Figure 4). The subregion's upper middle-income and high-income DMCs have vaccinated an average of 57% of their total population, while the comparable figure for lower middle-income to low-income countries is around 20%.

Figure 3: Growth Forecasts versus Vaccination Coverage

GDP growth,
2019-2021

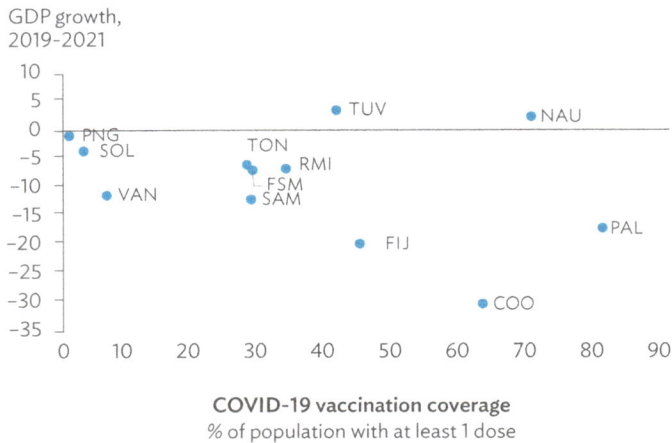

COVID-19 vaccination coverage
% of population with at least 1 dose

COO = Cook Islands, COVID-19 = coronavirus disease, FIJ = Fiji,
FSM = Federated States of Micronesia, GDP = gross domestic product,
NAU = Nauru, PAL = Palau, PNG = Papua New Guinea, RMI = Republic of the
Marshall Islands, SAM = Samoa, SOL = Solomon Islands, TON = Tonga,
TUV = Tuvalu, VAN = Vanuatu, y-o-y = year-on-year.
Note: Data as of 21 June 2021.
Sources: M. Roser, H. Ritchie, E. Ortiz-Ospina, and J. Hasell. 2020. *Coronavirus
Pandemic (COVID-19)*. https://ourworldindata.org/coronavirus (accessed 23
July 2021); Pacific Data Hub. 2020. *COVID-19 vaccination*. https://pacificdata.
org (accessed 23 July 2021); Asian Development Outlook database (accessed
25 June 2021); authors' calculations.

Figure 4: Per Capita Income versus Vaccination Coverage

Per capita GDP,
2020 current $

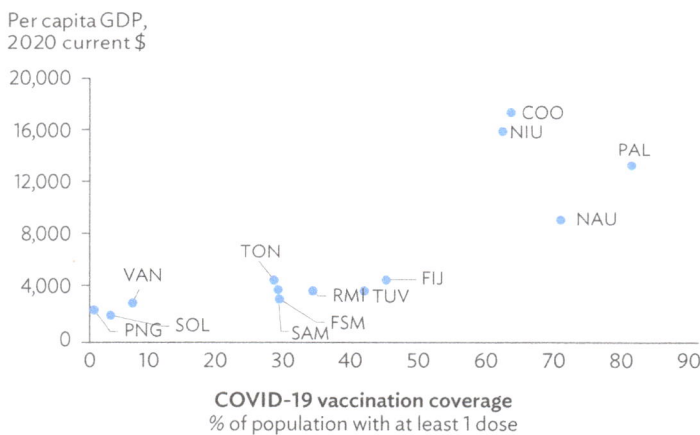

COVID-19 vaccination coverage
% of population with at least 1 dose

COO = Cook Islands, COVID-19 = coronavirus disease, FIJ = Fiji,
FSM = Federated States of Micronesia, GDP = gross domestic product,
NAU = Nauru, NIU = Niue, PAL = Palau, PNG = Papua New Guinea,
RMI = Republic of the Marshall Islands, SAM = Samoa, SOL = Solomon
Islands, TON = Tonga, TUV = Tuvalu, VAN = Vanuatu, y-o-y = year-on-year.
Note: Data as of 21 June 2021.
Sources: M. Roser, H. Ritchie, E. Ortiz-Ospina, and J. Hasell. 2020.
Coronavirus Pandemic (COVID-19). https://ourworldindata.org/coronavirus
(accessed 23 July 2021); Pacific Data Hub. 2020. *COVID-19 vaccination*.
https://pacificdata.org (accessed 23 July 2021); Asian Development Outlook
database (accessed 25 June 2021); and authors' calculations.

Although COVAX has been the main source of vaccines for many countries, supplies are severely limited, and deliveries have been delayed. Bilateral partners such as Australia, New Zealand, the US, India, Japan, and the People's Republic of China have also supported

vaccine procurements, assisted rollouts or, in some cases, subsumed the vaccination rollouts in associated Pacific DMCs under their own national programs. No Pacific DMC has engaged in direct bilateral agreements with vaccine manufacturers to date.

FACTORS AFFECTING VACCINE ROLLOUT

In addition to widely disparate population sizes and characteristics as well as degrees of geographic dispersion, the varying progress in COVID-19 vaccine rollout across the Pacific arises from a range of factors influencing a national health system's capacity to procure and distribute vaccines. This section broadly discusses selected areas where countries are known to be facing constraints.

Implementation-related issues. Many factors directly affect rollouts of the COVID-19 vaccine, from procurement to importation, distribution, and safe administration. This section draws heavily from country self-assessments conducted in the first quarter of 2021 using the Vaccine Introduction Readiness Assessment Tool/Vaccine Readiness Assessment Framework 2.0, a tool jointly developed by the United Nations Children's Fund, the World Bank, and WHO to help countries assess their capacity to deliver the vaccine and identify gaps requiring additional action. The issues highlighted below are a selection of the full set covered by the assessment tool.

- **Vaccine access.** Support from bilateral partners comes at varying speeds, affecting vaccine rollouts in countries depending on them. Meanwhile, many Pacific countries have initially relied on the COVAX facility for their vaccine supply, and they face uncertainties about the vaccine shelf life, and delayed shipments. Also, with some bilateral governments providing donations only of selected vaccines, the recipient country must ensure that the vaccine donated can be distributed by its health system.

  While COVAX has committed to supply doses to up to 20% coverage to Gavi's Advance Market Commitment (AMC) countries,[2] which are the low- and middle-income economies receiving subsidized vaccines through COVAX AMC, several Pacific DMCs are yet to receive the committed volume of doses because of continued delayed shipments and global shortages.[3] Beyond the initial 20% coverage, COVAX is also offering countries access to cost-shared doses, and the initial offering for both Moderna and Johnson & Johnson doses are for delivery in the fourth quarter of 2021 through the second and third quarters of 2022. However, the exact cost-sharing and procurement mechanism remains to be confirmed.

  It must also be noted that the WHO's Roadmap for Prioritizing Uses of COVID-19 Vaccines in the Context of Limited Supply prioritizes vaccinations in places with widespread transmission. This means that Pacific countries which have thus far successfully stayed free of COVID-19 may have to wait longer to receive shipments from COVAX than countries battling outbreaks.

- **Resourcing.** Countries across the subregion are doing their best to plan COVID-19 vaccine rollouts, but uncertainties in timelines may cause some difficulty in ensuring that sufficient resources are available to support vaccine rollout when supplies do arrive. This is particularly challenging with the COVID-19 vaccine because, for many Pacific DMCs, it will be the first vaccine to be introduced to the adult population and therefore requires new distribution channels. Other cost requirements, such as those for proper waste management, must also be estimated.

The unknowns on the expenditure side are accompanied by ongoing fiscal constraints. Grant financing from development partners has helped reduce the need to take on additional borrowing, but for countries with less access to such funding, the increased costs from supporting a COVID-19 response have had serious implications on their debt portfolios (a discussion on the impact of grants on the debt trajectories of Samoa and Tonga is on pages 22-23).

- **Supply chain management.** Most Pacific countries have indicated preference for the COVID-19 vaccines that can be stored at 2°C–8°C range, reflecting the level of cold chain equipment most widely available in the subregion. Ultra-cold chain equipment, for vaccines that must be stored at subzero temperatures, is in much shorter supply or even unavailable in some cases. These types of vaccines can be stored using dry ice, but a sustainable supply of the substance will be required for this option to be viable.

The capacity of a country's cold chain system can also become an issue. For example, an initial assessment estimates that Samoa has sufficient space (at 2°C–8°C) nationwide to store COVID-19 vaccines for inoculating 20% of its population, but shortages may emerge if target coverage is increased to 60%, as is expected to happen when the vaccine is rolled out to more of the population. Further, since most immunization vaccines used in the Pacific are also stored at these temperatures, staggering and other stock management measures will be needed during high-volume periods (e.g., school catch-up vaccinations). There are also concerns in other countries about cold chain storage at the provincial and local levels not meeting WHO standards or not functioning at all. Expanding storage capacity (e.g., by constructing new facilities or procuring additional cold chain equipment) will take time and likely require funding support. This would also entail increased costs for maintenance and procurement of standby power supplies to ensure the continued viability of the expanded system.

- **Service delivery.** Logistics also pose a significant challenge to comprehensive health service delivery in the Pacific countries with remote outer island communities. For example, Tonga's Ha'apai island group consists of small islands widely dispersed over the open sea. Related matters to consider include availability of both maritime and land transport, fuel for transportation and power supply, and securing adequate space for vaccination sites. Ideally, sites would be set up in large, open areas, such as community or church halls, that can service large groups of people but still allow for social distancing. In addition, registration of all persons receiving the vaccine and careful record-keeping of vaccination details will be crucial in post-immunization monitoring.

- **Human resources and training.** Ensuring that there will be enough trained health care professionals at vaccination sites is proving to be an issue in the Pacific. Across the subregion, nurses are usually responsible for administering vaccines, and the need to immunize large segments of the population nationwide is exposing staffing shortages, especially outside major urban centers. In Tonga, nurses from the main island of Tongatapu will provide reinforcements in the outer islands, while Vanuatu plans to mobilize retired nurses to supplement its active workforce. Tuvalu does not have enough nurses locally and is engaging nurses from Fiji and Kiribati.

Pacific countries also recognize the need to train health and other essential workers joining the vaccination teams. However, country self-assessments point to delays in developing and conducting the needed training programs, including hands-on modules and drills. Further training and orientation will be needed once the countries have more information on the type of vaccine they will be handling. Several Pacific countries have previously received the AstraZeneca vaccine through COVAX AMC described above and expressed reservations at potentially introducing different vaccines in limited and already stretched immunization programs.

- **Post-vaccination considerations.** The management of hazardous medical waste is an important consideration given COVID-19's infectious nature. Proper on-site waste management and access to incinerators will be crucial. Tuvalu has reported that the incinerator for the Princess Margaret Hospital, the only incinerator on the mainland, has malfunctioned, so medical waste is being burned using diesel fuel in empty kerosene drums, posing serious health and environmental risks.

This area also covers post-vaccination monitoring and surveillance, including management of any adverse events following immunization (AEFIs) that, if left unaddressed, may alarm the public and contribute to vaccine hesitancy. Thus, there is the need to ensure that vaccination sites have sufficient medication, equipment, and trained personnel to respond quickly to any emergencies. Many countries have requested to receive only one type of vaccine to minimize challenges in AEFI surveillance; those that will accept more than one type, such as Samoa, will have to undertake additional measures to mitigate a broader range of AEFIs.

Vaccine hesitancy. Achieving collective ("herd") immunity from COVID-19, wherein enough of the population becomes immune to the disease and transmission thus becomes unlikely, faces a serious challenge from those who might choose to delay their vaccination or refuse it outright. Some may want to wait until more knowledge is available about the effects of COVID-19 vaccines before deciding whether to be immunized, while others hold negative personal views of vaccinations in general or the COVID-19 vaccine in particular.

Misinformation is contributing to this hesitancy and may also endanger public health by promoting practices that are ineffective against COVID-19 or can even be harmful. Although the decision whether to receive the vaccination remains a personal one, providing access to relevant, timely, and accurate information about the COVID-19 vaccine is key to helping everyone make truly informed decisions. Countries across the Pacific recognize the need to raise this sort of awareness, as well as to be prepared to address public concerns about AEFIs.

Fragility and vulnerability to disasters. Political instability and weak governance are likely to further affect the efficiency of service delivery, and damage from disasters and adverse impacts of climate change—to which the Pacific is especially vulnerable—place added strain on limited resources and logistical chains. Tropical Cyclone Harold, which struck the subregion in April 2020, had damaged cold chain equipment in Vanuatu, adding to the costs and considerations of the country's COVID-19 response plan.

CONCLUSION AND RECOMMENDATIONS

The arrival of COVID-19 on Pacific shores, with the subregion's most populous countries contending with local outbreaks, and the pandemic's severe impact on economic growth makes protection against COVID-19 through immunization urgent. Vaccination against COVID-19 has begun all over the Pacific, but with varying degrees of progress. Country preparedness, accessibility of vaccine supply, community vaccine acceptance, and logistics differ across countries.

Development partners will continue to play a crucial role. Their resources and expertise will aid in funding and facilitating procurement, especially for countries with limited purchasing power. Aside from vaccine procurement, development partners should continue to strengthen the capacity of the health systems to safely introduce new vaccines. They will also have the networks and mechanisms for coordinating and cooperating with other partners, providing similar assistance in the subregion towards efficiently broadening vaccine coverage.

Investments in cold chain equipment and supply chain management are still required in some Pacific countries to ensure they can safely store and deliver sufficient stocks of the COVID-19 vaccine. Development partner investments in energy, transport, and trade facilitation would also support supply management and delivery efforts.

Further, adequate training is critical to ensure that health care professionals and related essential workers effectively play their respective roles in immunizing the public against COVID-19 and assisting them through any AEFIs. Investing in digital management solutions and governance would also help strengthen the health sector's overall capacity and facilitate data collection and management in support of policymaking. Budgeting for operation and maintenance and accounting for disaster risk mitigation are also important for continuity in service, as the task of vaccinating populations will take time.

Health systems need to continue to invest and strengthen their routine outreach and immunization programs. This will ensure that the rollout of the COVID-19 vaccine does not displace routine childhood immunization and introduction of other new vaccines. Other areas not limited to those discussed above, such as safety surveillance, waste management, and regulatory reform, should also not be neglected.

Addressing vaccine hesitancy calls for stronger communications between governments and their constituents. This would involve the dissemination of timely and accurate information; counteract misinformation, especially that regarding vaccine safety and managing of AEFIs; and promote general vaccine literacy. Collaboration with nongovernment and community-based organizations and local leaders, whether by governments or development partners, should facilitate direct engagement with the public and build demand for and trust in the COVID-19 vaccine.

Lead authors: Kelvin Lam, Inez Mikkelsen-Lopez, Remrick Patagan, and Cara Tinio.

Endnotes

[1] SBS News. 2021. *Fiji fears a coronavirus 'tsunami' after outbreak found to be Indian variant.* https://www.sbs.com.au/news/fiji-fears-a-coronavirus-tsunami-after-outbreak-found-to-be-indian-variant. 28 April.

[2] Gavi, the Vaccine Alliance, is co-leading the COVAX facility. For further information, see gavi.org.

[3] J. Hollingsworth. 2021. *The world's biggest vaccine maker is stalling on exports. That's a problem for the planet's most vulnerable.* CNN. 26 May.

References

Asian Development Bank (ADB). 2021. *Pacific Approach 2021–2025.* Manila.

ADB. 2021. *Report and Recommendation of the President to the Board of Directors: Proposed Grants for Additional Financing to the Independent State of Samoa, the Kingdom of Tonga, Tuvalu, and the Republic of Vanuatu for the Systems Strengthening for Effective Coverage of New Vaccines in the Pacific Project under the Asia Pacific Vaccine Access Facility.* Vaccine Needs Assessment: Samoa (accessible from the list of linked documents in Appendix 2). Manila.

ADB. 2021. *Report and Recommendation of the President to the Board of Directors: Proposed Grants for Additional Financing to the Independent State of Samoa, the Kingdom of Tonga, Tuvalu, and the Republic of Vanuatu for the Systems Strengthening for Effective Coverage of New Vaccines in the Pacific Project under the Asia Pacific Vaccine Access Facility.* Vaccine Needs Assessment: Tonga (accessible from the list of linked documents in Appendix 2). Manila.

ADB. 2021. *Report and Recommendation of the President to the Board of Directors: Proposed Grants for Additional Financing to the Independent State of Samoa, the Kingdom of Tonga, Tuvalu, and the Republic of Vanuatu for the Systems Strengthening for Effective Coverage of New Vaccines in the Pacific Project under the Asia Pacific Vaccine Access Facility.* Vaccine Needs Assessment: Tuvalu (accessible from the list of linked documents in Appendix 2). Manila.

ADB. *2021. Report and Recommendation of the President to the Board of Directors: Proposed Grants for Additional Financing to the Independent State of Samoa, the Kingdom of Tonga, Tuvalu, and the Republic of Vanuatu for the Systems Strengthening for Effective Coverage of New Vaccines in the Pacific Project under the Asia Pacific Vaccine Access Facility.* Vaccine Needs Assessment: Vanuatu (accessible from the list of linked documents in Appendix 2). Manila.

McGarry, D. 2021. Vanuatu coronavirus vaccine rollout to take until end of 2023. *The Guardian.* 25 February.

Natalegawa, A. and C. Bismonte. 2021. A Patchwork Vaccine Rollout in the Pacific Islands. *The Diplomat.* 19 March.

Pacific Data Hub. 2020. *COVID-19 vaccination.* https://pacificdata.org (accessed 25 June 2021).

Roser, M., H. Ritchie, E. Ortiz-Ospina, and J. Hasell. 2020. *Coronavirus Pandemic (COVID-19).* https://ourworldindata.org/coronavirus (accessed 25 June 2021).

Tinio, C., R. Rabanal, I. Mikkelsen-Lopez, K. Lam. 2021. The Pacific: Crossing "the Last Mile." In ADB. *Asian Economic Integration Report 2021: Making Digital Platforms Work for Asia and the Pacific.* Manila.

Worldometer COVID-19 Data (accessed 25 June 2021).

Beyond COVID-19: Learning and earning losses from school closures

One of the sectors hit hardest by the coronavirus disease (COVID-19) pandemic is education. Movement restrictions imposed by governments across the world have included the suspension of physical class meetings and a shift to distance learning to minimize the disruption to education. Although the extent of school closures has been less in the Pacific developing member countries (DMCs) than in other subregions, they still have had an impact on both the learning and potential earnings of Pacific students. And these impacts can be magnified given the inherent vulnerabilities of the subregion, especially if infrastructure deficits remained unaddressed.

COVID-19 AND SCHOOL CLOSURES IN ASIA AND THE PACIFIC

The pandemic led to school disruptions in many parts of the world. These disruptions raise concern over the long-term welfare of students whose education is temporarily put on hold or reconfigured into a remote setup. By June 2021, schools had been closed for about 1 year or more in 13 of 46 economies in developing Asia. In eight other economies in the region, schools had been closed for 200–300 days. Most economies in developing Asia either implemented full closure of all schools or partial closures, where schools were closed only in certain regions or for some grade levels and age groups. School closures in countries like Bangladesh and the Philippines have lasted for more than 300 days. In many countries, schools have combined reduced class time with distance learning (UNESCO 2021).

However, the inherent geographical remoteness of Pacific DMCs, combined with their governments' prompt action to close ports of entry to their territories, have kept the number of COVID-19 cases low compared to the rest in developing Asia and allowed most schools to stay open. Schools in the subregion have been fully closed for an average of 32 days and partially closed for an average of 13 days only. Most Pacific DMCs started closing schools in March–April 2020. However, schools had resumed operations in all Pacific DMCs by July 2020, whether in full capacity or in part (Figure 1).

Research suggests that disruptions to education, such as school closures, adversely affect the learning progress of students. Students lose opportunities to acquire essential skills and may forget some of those they have learned after a break from school (Cooper et al. 1996). The skills they learn at earlier ages become a steppingstone to learn more advanced skills at a later age. Those who miss out on opportunities learning these skills at younger age are at risk of acquiring lower total skill levels in their lifetime (Meyers and Thomasson 2017; Gibbs et al. 2019; and Andrabi, Daniels, and Das 2020).

Figure 1: Status of Schools in Pacific Developing Member Countries, March–December 2020

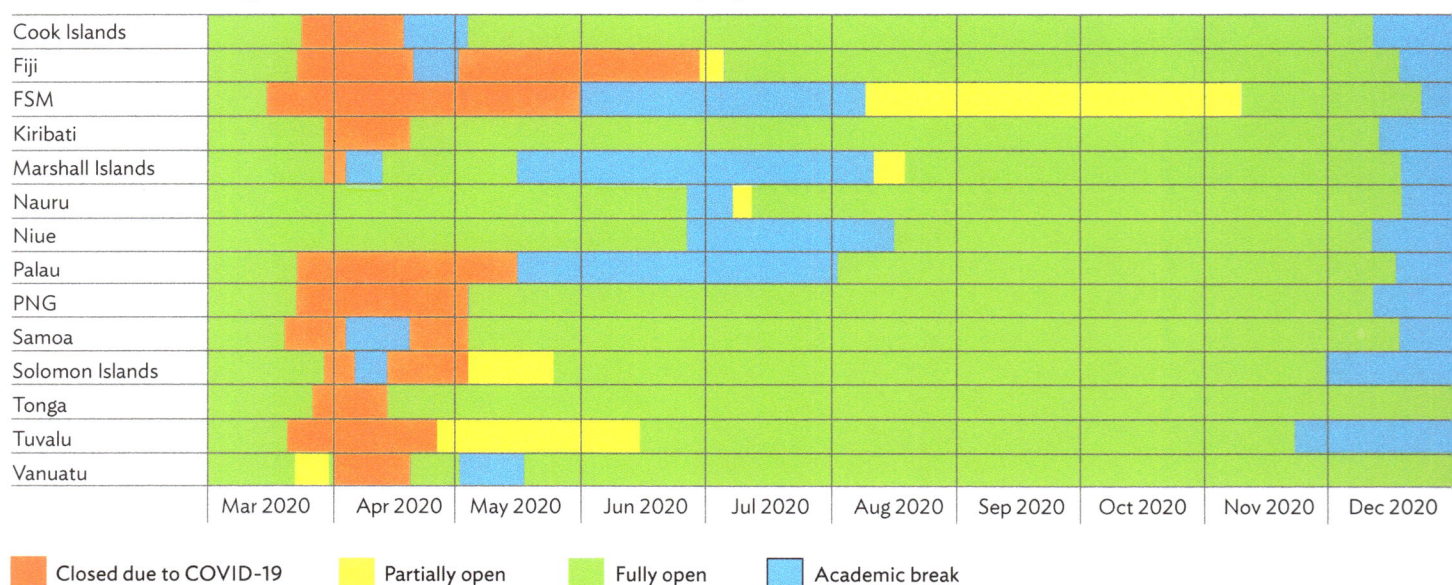

COVID-19 = coronavirus disease, FSM = Federated States of Micronesia, PNG = Papua New Guinea.
Source: UNESCO. *COVID-19 Education Response.* https://en.unesco.org/covid19/educationresponse (accessed 30 March 2021).

DISTANCE LEARNING STRATEGIES USED

A survey of education ministry officials conducted by UNESCO, UNICEF, and the World Bank from April to October 2020 shows that online and take-home modules have been the primary modes of instruction in Pacific DMCs during the school closures (Table 1). Out of the four modes of distance learning available in the Pacific, all Pacific DMCs except Niue used online platforms to continue the classes disrupted by the pandemic. Given the geographical remoteness of many of the Pacific DMCs, distance learning via online platform provided the widest coverage for many students. Pacific islanders often do not have access to TV or radio because of limited TV/radio stations and frequencies. Distribution of take-home learning packages can be difficult and expensive outside the main islands in the absence of reliable delivery services and logistics support.

The sudden closure of schools because of the COVID-19 pandemic meant that teachers and primary caregivers (usually parents) had little time to prepare for distance learning. Many teachers had to reorient themselves and overhaul their teaching strategies to conform with distance learning platforms. To help teachers in Pacific DMCs transition into their new role, they were provided with teaching content from open educational resources (UNESCO, UNICEF, and World Bank 2020). Caregivers needed to juggle supervising their children's distance learning with other responsibilities, such as housework and working from home. Some governments in the Pacific helped them by giving guidance materials for home-based learning (UNESCO, UNICEF, and World Bank 2020).

ACCESS TO DISTANCE LEARNING

Access to distance learning depends on households having the necessary equipment. The majority of households in Pacific DMCs cannot access distance education via computers. Only 11% of households in Papua New Guinea have computer access, and only 31% in Kiribati and Samoa.

Households are further constrained from online learning by lack of internet access. Only 4% of households in Samoa have internet access and only 47% in Kiribati, compared with a 60% average for developing Asia. In nearly every Pacific DMC, less than half of the population have ever used the internet (Figure 2). This level of online literacy rendered the Pacific unprepared for this mode of instruction.

While almost every household in developing Asia has a mobile phone, only 56% of homes in Papua New Guinea and 68% in Kiribati have one. On average, only 7 in 10 persons in the Pacific are using a mobile phone. Less than half of the populations in the Federated States of Micronesia, Kiribati, the Marshall Islands, and Papua New Guinea are subscribed to mobile cellular services (Figure 3).

Figure 2: Individuals Using the Internet, 2017

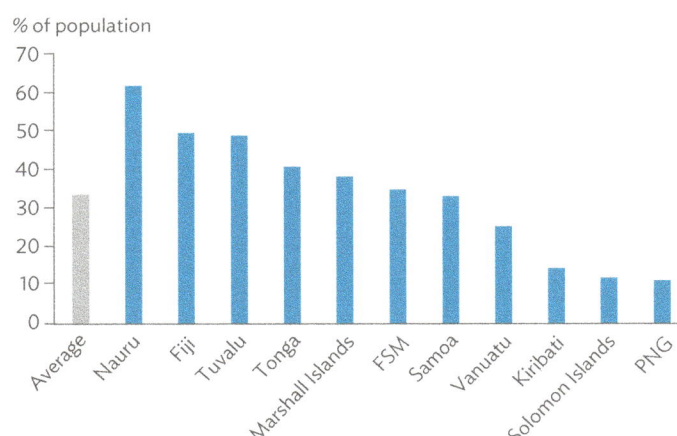

FSM = Federated States of Micronesia; PNG = Papua New Guinea.
Note: No data are available for the Cook Islands, Niue, and Palau.
Source: World Development Indicators.

Table 1: Remote Learning Modes Used by Pacific Developing Member Countries

Country	Survey Month	Online Platforms	Television	Radio	Take-Home Packages
Cook Islands	July	√			√
Fiji	April, May, or June	√	√	√	√
Kiribati	April, May, or June	√			
Niue	April, May, or June				√
Palau	April, May, or June	√			√
PNG	April, May, or June	√	√	√	
Samoa	October	√	√	√	
Solomon Islands	August	√	√	√	√
Tonga	July	√	√	√	√
Tuvalu	August	√	√	√	√
Vanuatu	August	√	√	√	√

PNG = Papua New Guinea.
Note: No data are available for the Federated States of Micronesia, the Marshall Islands, and Nauru.
Source: ADB (2021) based on UNESCO, UNICEF, and the World Bank. 2020. *Survey on National Education Responses to COVID-19 School Closures, Round 1 (April–June) and Round 2 (July–October)*. http://tcg.uis.unesco.org/survey-education-covid-school-closures/ (accessed 13 April 2021).

Figure 3: Mobile Cellular Subscriptions, 2017

per 100 people

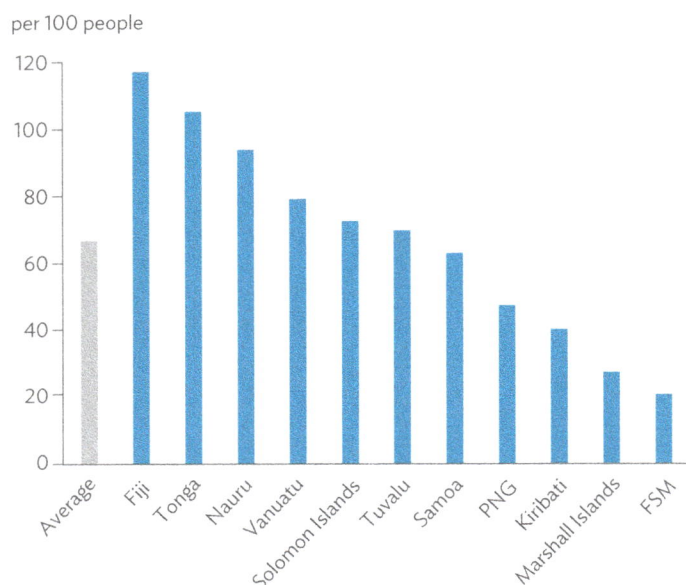

FSM = Federated States of Micronesia; PNG = Papua New Guinea.
Note: No data are available for the Cook Islands, Niue, and Palau.
Source: World Development Indicators.

LEARNING LOSSES

There are three factors that make instruction under this remote setup less effective than face-to-face learning—its "unplanned nature, the involvement of younger-age children, and distractions at home that keep children from being able to focus on studying"

(ADB 2021). Moreover, access to distance learning equipment is limited. Thus, students incurred losses in learning during this period of school closures. The magnitude of these losses depended on the length of school closures as well as the effectiveness of distance strategies used. Three scenarios on the effectiveness of distance learning are considered—optimistic, intermediate, and pessimistic—and described in detail in ADB (2021).

On average, countries in the Pacific subregion lost 8.0% of a year of learning (ADB 2021), equivalent to a full month's worth of learning. This was equivalent to 1.3% of the 6.6 years of learning that people in the Pacific acquired on average before the pandemic. Learning losses were highest in the Federated States of Micronesia (3.4 months of learning), where schools have been partially or fully closed the longest. Fiji lost 2.0 months of learning and Tuvalu 1.2 months. Palau and Papua New Guinea each lost 1.1 months of learning. The rest of the Pacific DMCs lost less than 1 month of learning (Figure 4).

By keeping schools mostly open, Pacific DMCs have kept learning losses at bay. Even in the least-effective scenario of distance learning, the subregion lost only 1.3 months of learning, or 1.7% of the average months of learning in 2020. This is a far cry from the average learning losses in the rest of developing Asia.[1] In South Asia, where school closures have reached about 1 year, learning losses were equivalent to 6.6 months of learning, or 8.6% of the average months of learning that people in South Asia acquired before the pandemic. Learning losses in East Asia reached 4.7, in Southeast Asia reached 4.2, and in Central Asia 2.9 months of learning (ADB 2021). If school closures in Pacific DMCs were extended, it would result in more losses in learning.

Figure 4: Months of Learning Lost in Pacific Developing Member Countries Because of School Closures

Months

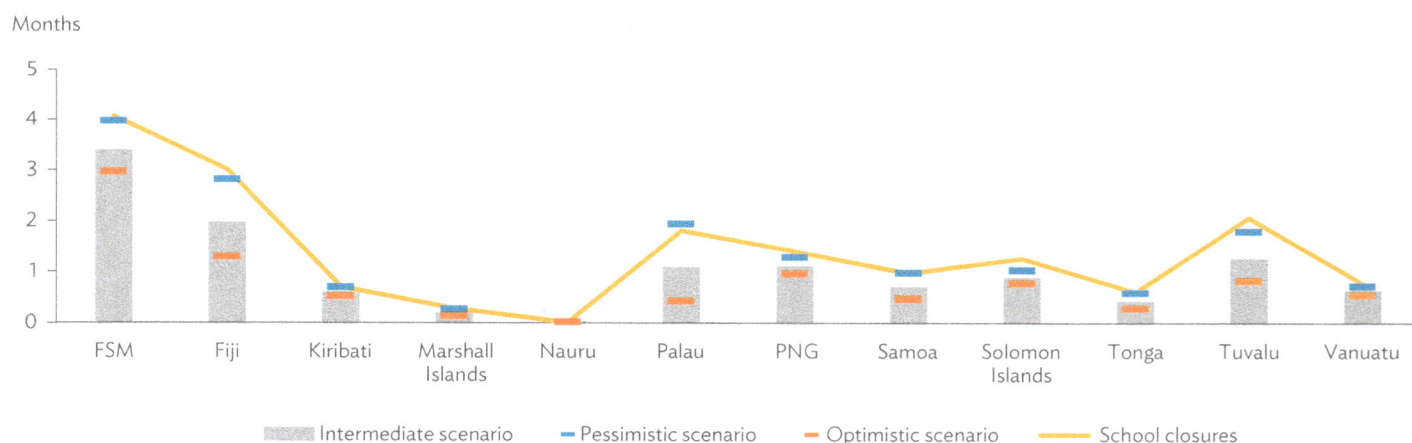

FSM = Federated States of Micronesia, PNG = Papua New Guinea.
Notes:
1. School closures are the number of days that schools are partially or fully closed, normalized by 365 days.
2. Each day of partial closure is assumed to be equivalent to half a day of full closure.
3. No data are available for Cook Islands and Niue.
Source: ADB. 2021. Learning and Earning Losses from COVID-19 School Closures in Developing Asia. *Asian Development Outlook 2021: Financing a Green and Inclusive Recovery.* Manila.

LOSSES IN POTENTIAL EARNINGS

Learning losses will influence the skills of students affected by school closures. In turn, this will affect their productivity in the future. In the long run, closure of schools in the Pacific during 2020 is estimated to result in a loss in future earnings equivalent to $42 per year for every student affected (Table 2). This is a 0.6% decline in their expected annual earnings. Over the lifetime of these students, the losses accrue to about $247 million in present-value terms, equivalent to 3.7% of the subregion's GDP in 2020. Developing Asia stands to lose a total of $1.25 trillion in lifetime earnings of students affected by school closures. This is equivalent to 5.4% of the region's GDP in 2020 (ADB 2021).

If the relatively short closure of schools during the pandemic resulted in these losses in learning and potential earnings, then longer or more frequent disruptions because of disasters may result in even bigger losses accumulated over time. This is particularly true for Pacific DMCs which are highly vulnerable to such disasters. Since 2012, at least 10 tropical cyclones have struck these countries, resulting in massive damages to property, buildings, and infrastructure, aside from the lives lost.[2] In the absence of reliable alternative modes of learning, losses to learning and potential earnings would pile up.

MAKING EDUCATION RESILIENT

The disruption to education caused by the COVID-19 pandemic highlights the need for effective and reliable alternative learning approaches. As the Pacific subregion is vulnerable to disasters, disruptions to physical classes are a frequent occurrence. In this respect, information and communication technology (ICT) can play an important role in making education resilient. This latest episode of school closures, though relatively short, revealed the inherent weakness of Pacific education systems with the current state of its digital infrastructure unable to support the continuation of education through distance learning.

Internet connectivity has already improved in the Pacific. But while many Pacific DMCs are now able to connect to the internet, a lot more either do not have access at all or can only connect intermittently because of poor quality. Many citizens continue to rely on satellite technology for internet connection, which has been a major source for peoples residing in far flung islands, because of its broad coverage. However, submarine cables remain a more reliable source of internet and, until the projects in the pipeline are installed and become fully operational, many will continue to be excluded from enjoying fast and affordable internet services. This will continue to restrict students' access to viable distance learning.

Subsequently, accelerating the integration of ICT in education requires vital policy actions that will support it. These include supporting effective use of education management information systems, establishing a subregional e-learning resource center to achieve scale economies, and delivering ICT training programs for education stakeholders (ADB 2018b). Another important impediment to ICT's integration in education is the lack of technical know-how. Capacity-building both on the supply and demand sides of education, complemented by reliable digital infrastructure, will be necessary to improve the resiliency of education in the Pacific.

Table 2: Earning Losses in Selected Pacific Developing Member Countries

	Loss in Earnings per Student per Year (current $)			% Decline in Earnings per Student per Year			Baseline Average Earnings per Worker per Year (current $)	Loss in Lifetime Earnings (current $ million)		
	Optimistic	Intermediate	Pessimistic	Optimistic	Intermediate	Pessimistic		Optimistic	Intermediate	Pessimistic
Pacific	30	42	58	0.5	0.6	0.9	6,509	169	247	349
Fiji	69	104	150	1.1	1.6	2.3	6,403	133	201	289
Nauru	0	0	0	0.0	0.0	0.0	...	0	0	0
Samoa	23	34	49	0.4	0.6	0.8	6,005	10	14	20
Tonga	19	28	39	0.2	0.3	0.5	8,260	5	8	11
Vanuatu	26	30	35	0.5	0.6	0.6	5,368	22	24	28

... = data not available.
Note: No data are available for the Cook Islands, the Federated States of Micronesia, Kiribati, the Marshall Islands, Palau, Papua New Guinea, Solomon Islands, and Tuvalu.
Source: ADB. 2021. Learning and Earning Losses from COVID-19 School Closures in Developing Asia. *Asian Development Outlook 2021: Financing a Green and Inclusive Recovery*. Manila.

Lead authors: Rhea Molato-Gayares, Economic Research and Regional Cooperation Department, ADB, and Noel Del Castillo.

Endnotes

[1]   The Pacific subregion is part of the developing Asia based on ADB's classification.

[2]   Cyclones/typhoons Evan (2012), Haiyan (2013), Ian (2014), Ita (2014), Maysak (2015), Pam (2015), Winston (2016), Gita (2018), Harold (2020), and Yasa (2020) had an estimated total damage cost of at least $1.5 billion (ADB 2018a; Ravuwai 2020; and Talei 2021).

References

ADB. 2018a. *Asian Economic Integration Report 2018: Toward Optimal Provision of Regional Public Goods in Asia and the Pacific*. Manila.

ADB. 2018b. *ICT for Better Education in the Pacific*. Manila.

ADB. 2021. Learning and Earning Losses from COVID-19 School Closures in Developing Asia. *Asian Development Outlook 2021: Financing a Green and Inclusive Recovery*. Manila.

Andrabi, T., B. Daniels, and J. Das. 2020. Human Capital Accumulation and Disasters: Evidence from the Pakistan Earthquake of 2005. *RISE Working Paper Series* No. 20/039. Research on Improving Systems of Education Programme. https://doi.org/10.35489/BSG-RISE-WP_2020/039.

Australian Strategic Policy Institute. 2020. *ICT for Development in the Pacific Islands: An Assessment of E-government capabilities in Fiji, Papua New Guinea, Samoa, Solomon Islands, Tonga and Vanuatu*. https://www.aspi.org.au/report/ict-development-pacific-islands.

Cooper, H. et al. 1996. The Effects of Summer Vacation on Achievement Test Scores: A Narrative and Meta-Analytic Review. *Review of Educational Research*. 66(3).

Gibbs, L. et al. 2019. Delayed Disaster Impacts on Academic Performance of Primary School Children. *Child Development*. 90(4).

Meyers, K. and M. Thomasson. 2017. Paralyzed by Panic: Measuring the Effect of School Closures during the 1916 Polio Pandemic on Educational Attainment. *NBER Working Paper* No. 23890. National Bureau of Economic Research.

Ravuwai, I. 2020. Estimated Damage from Cyclone Harold is $100M, Minister Says. *Fiji Sun*. 28 May. https://fijisun.com.fj/2020/05/28/estimated-damage-from-cyclone-harold-is-100m-minister-says/.

Talei, F. 2021. Cyclone Yasa Damage Costs Hit $500m: Seruiratu. *Fiji Sun*. 13 February. https://fijisun.com.fj/2021/02/13/cyclone-yasa-damage-costs-hit-500m-seruiratu/.

UNESCO. 2021. Monitoring COVID-19 Caused Closures of Educational Institutions. *Education Sector Methodological Note*. 20 January. https://en.unesco.org/covid19/educationresponse.

UNESCO, UNICEF, and World Bank. 2020. *Survey on National Education Responses to COVID-19 School Closures, Round 1 (April–June) and Round 2 (July–October)*. http://tcg.uis.unesco.org/%20survey-education-covid-school-closures/ (accessed 13 April 2021).

ADB's new development strategy for its 12 smallest Pacific island developing member countries

The Asian Development Bank (ADB) began its engagement in the Pacific in 1966 when Samoa became its first developing member country in the subregion. Since then, ADB has grown to be the largest development partner (by lending volume) in the Pacific. Today, ADB supports 14 Pacific island countries with a total active loan and grant portfolio of $2.5 billion as of 15 July 2021, including $390.0 million from cofinancing from partners and other special funds.

Although each of ADB's Pacific developing member countries has its own unique cultural identity and economic structure, the subregion's 12 smallest Pacific island countries (the PIC-12) share a number of structural similarities.[1] In order to deliver efficient support and leverage opportunities for collaboration, ADB has adopted a differentiated approach to planning and implementing assistance for the PIC-12. In June 2021 ADB's Board of Directors generally endorsed the Pacific Approach 2021–2025 as ADB's country partnership strategy for the PIC-12.[2] The new Pacific Approach is designed to respond to the critical challenges brought on by the coronavirus disease (COVID-19), while also supporting the PIC-12 to build resilience and drive more inclusive and sustainable growth in years to come. It provides a unified strategy for the PIC-12 and helps to maximize opportunities for regional cooperation, operational efficiency, and development effectiveness. Further, it deepens partnerships between ADB, its development partners, and stakeholders across the PIC-12.

CORE DEVELOPMENT CHALLENGES

As a group of remote, sparsely populated island nations, the PIC-12 experience similar underlying pressures. They are all categorized as small island developing states (SIDS) (Figure 1). Further, although ADB classifies only six of the PIC-12 as fragile and conflict affected situation (FCAS) states, they all experience varying degrees of fragility.[3] The features of smallness, isolation, and dispersion common among the PIC-12 lead to five underlying barriers to socioeconomic development: (i) capacity and governance constraints, (ii) narrow economies that are vulnerable to shocks, (iii) high-cost structures, (iv) unequal access to services and opportunity, and (v) distance from major markets. These barriers culminate into three development challenges, which form the basis of ADB's strategy for the subregion.

Challenge 1: Vulnerability to shocks. The pandemic has emphasized the vulnerability of the PIC-12 to external shocks by highlighting structural challenges. Underlying pressures include narrow economic bases, import dependence, high exposure to hazards, and capacity constraints. Small economic bases translate to limited capacity to generate revenue, and hence limited fiscal space to take on debt. Narrow revenue sources, paired with economic volatility, jeopardize repayment capacity; and borrowing needs linked to COVID-19 may exacerbate debt sustainability concerns.

Their narrow economic bases create additional layers of exposure to international price fluctuations and other economic disruptions. Crucially, their low elevations, atoll topography, and placement along the Pacific Ring of Fire and the Pacific Cyclone belt set the PIC-12 apart as some of the most exposed nations, globally, to disasters and the impacts of climate change and variability. Although the PIC-12 are highly exposed to shocks, they have severely limited resources to prepare for and respond to them.

Challenge 2: Weak service delivery. Distance from major markets and limited economies of scale make it costly to build and operate essential infrastructure, like energy, water, and transport. At the same time, the internal dispersion of islands and populations in the PIC-12 create barriers to the provision of services. Outward migration and small populations lead to thin capacity to manage and maintain infrastructure across the subregion, contributing to the poor performance of utilities and state-owned enterprises (SOEs). Accordingly, the PIC-12 require support in constructing infrastructure and building the capacity to operate it on a commercial basis. Sound commercial management is increasingly important amid slowing demand for services atop drops in tourism arrivals.

Challenge 3: Slow growth. The PIC-12 economies are typically dominated by public expenditures, and the public sector is often the lead employer. Barriers to private sector growth include small domestic markets and lack of export opportunities, paired with structural constraints such as (i) high costs of doing business and complicated regulations; (ii) limited infrastructure and service to support business growth, such as transport and digital connectivity; and (iii) poor access to finance for micro, small, and medium-sized enterprises. At the same time, there are acute skills shortages, and public sectors in the PIC-12 provide limited formal social protection. The PIC-12 will benefit from immediate assistance to strengthen education and skills training systems, as well as support to increase social protection, particularly for vulnerable groups. Ongoing assistance to increase private sector participation and manage productive resources, like fisheries, will be essential for driving more inclusive and sustainable economic growth.

DEVELOPMENT OUTLOOK AND STRATEGY OBJECTIVES

COVID-19 impacts. The pandemic represents a severe shock to the PIC-12. While most have avoided its direct health impacts, the pandemic emphasized the need to strengthen health systems and buffers against economic shocks. The PIC-12 were among the first countries to fully close their borders; however, health safety has come at a high socioeconomic cost with the PIC-12 economies contracting by a weighted average of 5.8% in 2020. Minimal growth of 0.3% is projected for 2021.

Figure 1: Core Development Challenges in the 12 Smallest Pacific Island Countries

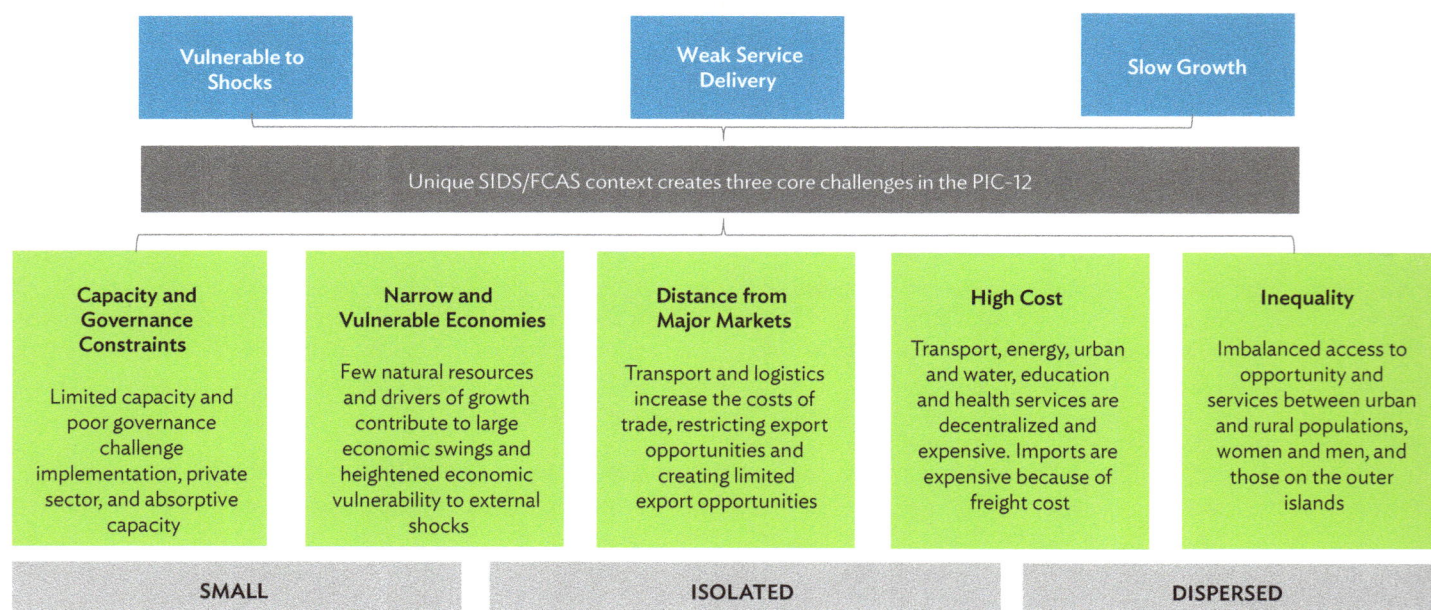

PIC-12 = 12 smallest Pacific island countries (the Cook Islands, the Federated States of Micronesia, Kiribati, the Marshall Islands, Nauru, Niue, Palau, Samoa, Solomon Islands, Tonga, Tuvalu, and Vanuatu); SIDS/FCAS = small island developing states/fragile and conflict-affected situations.
Source: ADB. 2021. *Pacific Approach, 2021–2025*. Manila. https://www.adb.org/sites/default/files/institutional-document/712796/pacific-approach-2021-2025.pdf.

ADB's response. The Pacific Approach 2021–2025 is designed to respond to immediate recovery needs in the wake of COVID-19, while supporting the PIC-12 in strengthening forward growth fundamentals and resilience to shocks (Figure 2). ADB has delivered budget support through its COVID-19 Pandemic Response Option modality and will assist the PIC-12 in strengthening public financial management (PFM) to ensure that development impacts are sustainable. In addition, the new Pacific Approach responds to the core challenges described above, through its three guiding objectives: (i) preparing for and responding to shocks, (ii) delivering sustainable services, and (iii) supporting inclusive growth. The underlying goal of the new strategy is "supporting a resilient Pacific." The Pacific Approach is aligned with ADB's Strategy 2030,[4] and with the stated development plans of government counterparts in each of the PIC-12.

Objective 1: Preparing for and respond to shocks. ADB will support the PIC-12 in (i) economic resilience and PFM, (ii) health system strengthening, (iii) disaster risk reduction, and (iv) economic recovery. ADB will target economic resilience by supporting fiscal and debt management, improved revenue collection and/or mobilization, monetary policy, and SOE reforms. Support for PFM will include guidance on fiscal consolidation, revenue management, public expenditure management, domestic savings, and private sector resource mobilization to support growth. Economic recovery efforts will assist the PIC-12 in designing and implementing policies to help restore tourism markets and operate both safely and profitably under the "new normal," including through travel bubbles. In the health sector, ADB will help strengthen rural service delivery, upskill workers, strengthen digital information systems, and improve

sector governance and management. Recognizing that bilateral partners are supporting vaccination programs, ADB will coordinate health assistance to support full coverage across the subregion.

Climate and disaster resilience are at the core of ADB's work in the PIC-12, and the Pacific Approach will oversee a strategic shift in how ADB addresses climate challenges in the subregion, namely through more comprehensive planning and response. Key features of ADB's support will include (i) climate-proofing all investments; (ii) supporting countries to collect and analyze risk data, and to inform long-term planning; (iii) delivering quick-dispersing assistance in the wake of disasters; (iv) providing contingent finance and insurance mechanisms; (v) enabling the PIC-12 to access international climate finance, including the Green Climate Fund; and (vi) expanding climate change support from the project level to the country and subregional levels.

Objective 2: Delivering sustainable services. Access to basic infrastructure and services—including electricity, transport, information and communication technology, water, sanitation, and hygiene—underpins inclusive development. The PIC-12 need support to increase both the coverage and quality of basic infrastructure and services. ADB is supporting the PIC-12 to overcome the "build, neglect, rebuild" paradigm by providing long-term sector support to help finance, manage, and maintain assets sustainably. Support for SOE reforms will be of particular importance for building resilience and managing state resources during and after COVID-19 as utilities in the subregion may be confronted with new fiscal constraints, such as reduced demand for

Figure 2: ADB's Support Under the Pacific Approach 2021–2025

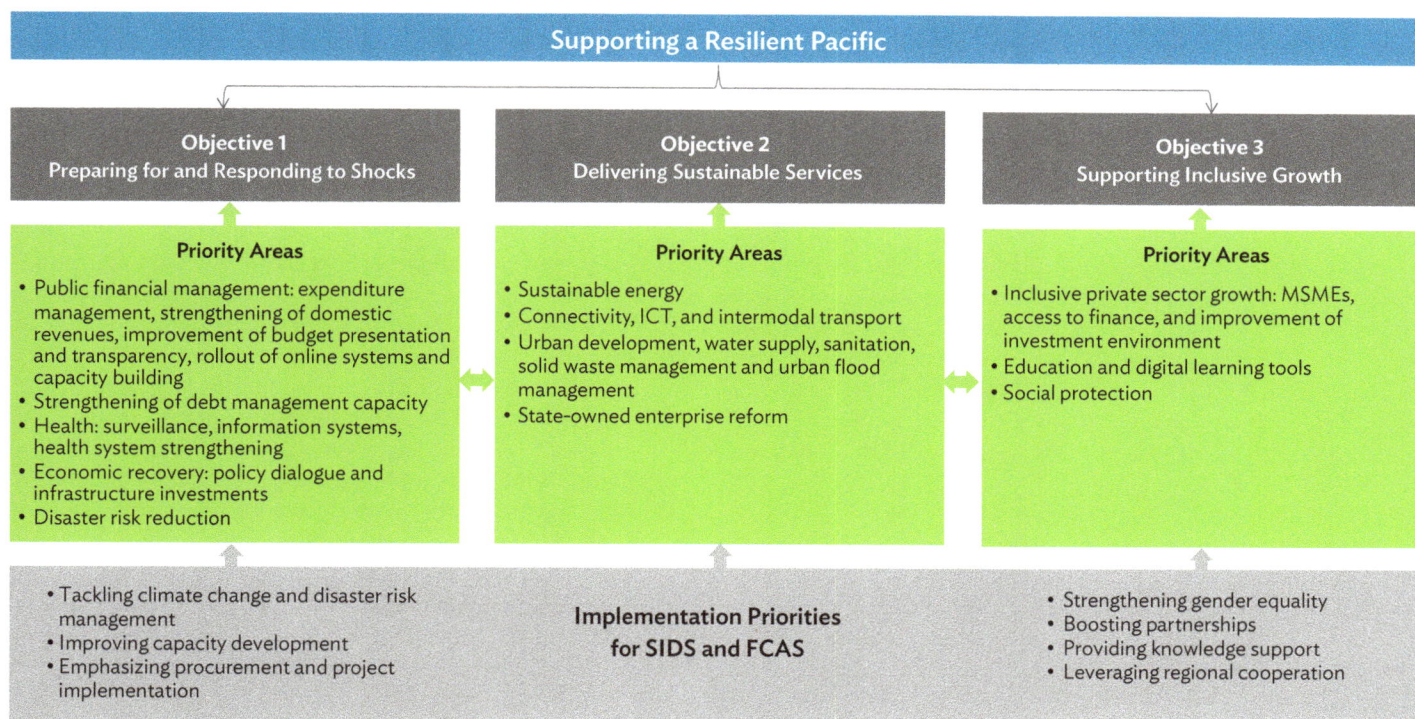

Supporting a Resilient Pacific

Objective 1 Preparing for and Responding to Shocks	**Objective 2** Delivering Sustainable Services	**Objective 3** Supporting Inclusive Growth
Priority Areas • Public financial management: expenditure management, strengthening of domestic revenues, improvement of budget presentation and transparency, rollout of online systems and capacity building • Strengthening of debt management capacity • Health: surveillance, information systems, health system strengthening • Economic recovery: policy dialogue and infrastructure investments • Disaster risk reduction	**Priority Areas** • Sustainable energy • Connectivity, ICT, and intermodal transport • Urban development, water supply, sanitation, solid waste management and urban flood management • State-owned enterprise reform	**Priority Areas** • Inclusive private sector growth: MSMEs, access to finance, and improvement of investment environment • Education and digital learning tools • Social protection
• Tackling climate change and disaster risk management • Improving capacity development • Emphasizing procurement and project implementation	**Implementation Priorities for SIDS and FCAS**	• Strengthening gender equality • Boosting partnerships • Providing knowledge support • Leveraging regional cooperation

ADB = Asian Development Bank, FCAS = fragile and conflict-affected situations; ICT = information and communication technology; MSMEs = micro, small, and medium-sized enterprises; SIDS = small island developing states.
Source: ADB. 2021. *Pacific Approach, 2021–2025*. Manila. https://www.adb.org/sites/default/files/institutional-document/712796/pacific-approach-2021-2025.pdf.

services linked to declines in tourist arrivals. Improving management practices, reforming institutions, and restructuring tariffs to enable cost-recovery will play an essential role in improving services and reducing the need for subsidies. ADB will continue to finance major civil works across sectors, promoting inclusive access to water, sanitation, solid waste disposal, transport, and electricity.

In the energy sector, ADB will help increase the share of renewable energy used for power generation by providing finance and technical assistance for solar, wind, and hydropower projects. Support will (i) improve energy efficiency, (ii) introduce battery storage, (iii) improve the technical and commercial performance of utilities, and (iv) enable public–private partnerships and increased private investment in clean energy. Transport operations account for more than half of ADB's Pacific portfolio in terms of lending volume, and ADB will continue to focus on roads, ports, and airports. ADB will increasingly provide sector lending and support long-term operation and maintenance, and scale up assistance to improve transport safety and security. Urban projects will focus on (i) improved urban services, (ii) forward-looking spatial planning, and (iii) environmental protection alongside urbanization.

Objective 3: Supporting inclusive growth. The Pacific Approach will strengthen foundations for growth across the subregion, increase ADB's direct engagement in PIC-12 private sectors, and scale up access to social protection services for vulnerable groups. ADB will address foundations for growth through several

complementary approaches. First, its Private Sector Development Initiative technical assistance will strengthen Pacific business environments through business law reforms, support for SOE and utility reforms, and by fostering the economic empowerment of women. Second, ADB will invest in education and skills training to promote equal access to opportunities and address persistent skills gaps affecting both the public and private sectors. Third, ADB will support the public sector to sustainably manage existing productive resources—such as fisheries and sovereign wealth funds—as well as identify new growth areas. Crucially, ADB will work with domestic and subregional entities to scale up access to finance for micro, small, and medium-sized enterprises.

ADB will increase its own engagement in the private sector by providing direct debt finance and making equity investments in commercially viable private sector projects across the PIC-12. ADB is implementing a new private sector strategy for the subregion focusing on renewable energy, financial institutions, tourism, and fisheries. The Asian Development Fund, through its Private Sector Window initiative, will encourage investment in markets experiencing disproportionate barriers to growth through co-investment and partnerships with commercial investors—targeting areas with high potential for positive social and environmental impacts. Complementing private sector support, ADB will implement a new social sector plan focusing on (i) improved access to high-quality social services, including health coverage and education; (ii) reduced vulnerability and enhanced resilience of poor and vulnerable groups, including through social protection support and enhanced income opportunities; and (iii) strengthened gender and social dimensions across all ADB's interventions. ADB will integrate social protection elements into its lending and technical assistance portfolios.

IMPLEMENTATION PRIORITIES

ADB's portfolio is expanding to meet the growing financing needs in the subregion. For the PIC-12, it is projected to grow from $568 million in 2015 to $1.6 billion in 2021.[5] The increase in financing requires innovation in the ways ADB implements its portfolio. Further, ADB's Strategy 2030 calls for differentiated approaches for SIDS and FCAS, recognizing their fragility and need to strengthen governance, institutions, and human capacity. Accordingly, the Pacific Approach focuses on improving efficiency and sustainability amid portfolio growth, and in the unique SIDS and FCAS operating environments.

ADB has seven priority areas for implementing the Pacific Approach. These seek to achieve complementarity across all stages of the project and portfolio life cycles by integrating country knowledge and local practices into project design, implementation, and portfolio management. ADB's implementation priorities will focus on deepening country knowledge; improving the effectiveness and efficiency of assistance; and strengthening cooperation at the national, subregional, and local levels. The implementation priorities are:

(i) **Addressing climate change and disaster risk management.** ADB has a new climate strategy for the subregion, which expands climate support from the project to the country level and will contribute to subregional interventions. The Pacific Approach will enable ADB to deliver more comprehensive support to build resilience across governments, communities, infrastructure, and economies in the PIC-12.

(ii) **Mainstreaming gender equity.** The Pacific Approach will ensure gender mainstreaming across ADB operations in the Pacific as well as support stand-alone gender initiatives in the areas of economic empowerment, human development, decision-making and leadership, time poverty, and resilience to shocks.

(iii) **Improving capacity.** ADB will scale up capacity building and use experts on a long-term basis to address skill gaps. It will establish a strategy for capacity support related to safeguards, and implement targeted subregional and country-specific capacity-building activities.

(iv) **Procurement innovation and project implementation.** ADB has begun piloting flexibilities to address bottlenecks in the subregion, including (a) removing contracting thresholds, (b) using joint selection between ADB and executing agencies, (c) using quality criteria on bid evaluation, (d) introducing flexible packaging to increase participation of domestic contractors and civil society organizations, and (e) expanding procurement guidance in FCAS. ADB will mainstream these innovations and explore new ones, such as the use of external agents for project implementation, and the introduction of subregional sector procurement plans.

(v) **Subregional cooperation.** ADB will deepen collaboration among the PIC-12 and explore subregional projects and technical assistance to deliver assistance more efficiently on a larger scale. It will also leverage subregional cooperation to create economies of scale—building on the success of a coordinated multi-country procurement model for vaccines[6]—and support the PIC-12 in establishing subregional public goods, such as the Pacific Energy Regulators Alliance, to build communities of best practice.

(vi) **Targeted knowledge support.** ADB will be selective in its approach to knowledge and capacity support, focusing implementation capacity and aligning knowledge activities with the objectives of the Pacific Approach. ADB will assist each PIC-12 to conduct country-specific fragility and sector assessments, and prepare voluntary national reviews to assess progress against the Sustainable Development Goals. ADB will provide knowledge solutions through its signature products—including the Private Sector Development Initiative and Pacific Economic Monitor—and develop new resources on specific topics, including women's economic empowerment.

(vii) **Enhancing partnerships.** ADB will continue to coordinate with development partners in the subregion while deepening national engagement and exploring partnerships with chambers of commerce, industry associations, academic institutions, think tanks, and civil society. ADB will work with partners to scale up cofinancing and strengthen coordination towards delivering transformative results on a larger scale.

The Pacific Approach builds on decades of experience partnering for development in the Pacific. It incorporates lessons from previous ADB planning documents, as well as hands-on work building infrastructure, supporting communities, and engaging with governments and partners in each of the PIC-12. The Pacific Approach will guide ADB's engagement in the subregion—supporting resilience and more inclusive growth across each of the PIC-12. ADB will continue to deepen its partnerships in the subregion, seeking to deliver more transformative results and sustainable impacts for people and communities across the Pacific.

Lead author: Roble Poe Velasco-Rosenheim.

Endnotes

1. The PIC-12 comprise the Cook Islands, the Federated States of Micronesia, Kiribati, the Marshall Islands, Nauru, Niue, Palau, Samoa, Solomon Islands, Tonga, Tuvalu, and Vanuatu. Niue became the newest ADB member in 2019.

2. ADB. 2021. *Pacific Approach, 2021—2025.* Manila. https://www.adb.org/sites/default/files/institutional-document/712796/pacific-approach-2021-2025.pdf.

3. As of December 2020, the PIC-12 FCAS countries are the Federated States of Micronesia, Kiribati, the Marshall Islands, Nauru, Solomon Islands, and Tuvalu. For more information on ADB's work with FCAS, see https://www.adb.org/fcas-sids-approach.

4. ADB. 2018. *Strategy 2030: Achieving a Prosperous, Inclusive, Resilient, and Sustainable Asia and the Pacific.* Manila. https://www.adb.org/documents/strategy-2030-prosperous-inclusive-resilient-sustainable-asia-pacific.

5. ADB. 2019. *Asian Development Fund (ADF) 13 Replenishment Meeting: A Framework for Addressing the Financing Needs of Small Island Developing States.* Manila.

6. ADB. 2018. *Report and Recommendation of the President to the Board of Directors: Proposed Loan and Grants to the Independent State of Samoa, the Kingdom of Tonga, Tuvalu, and the Republic of Vanuatu for the Systems Strengthening for Effective Coverage of New Vaccines in the Pacific Project.* Manila.

Nonfuel Merchandise Exports from Australia
(A$; y-o-y % change, 3-month m.a.)

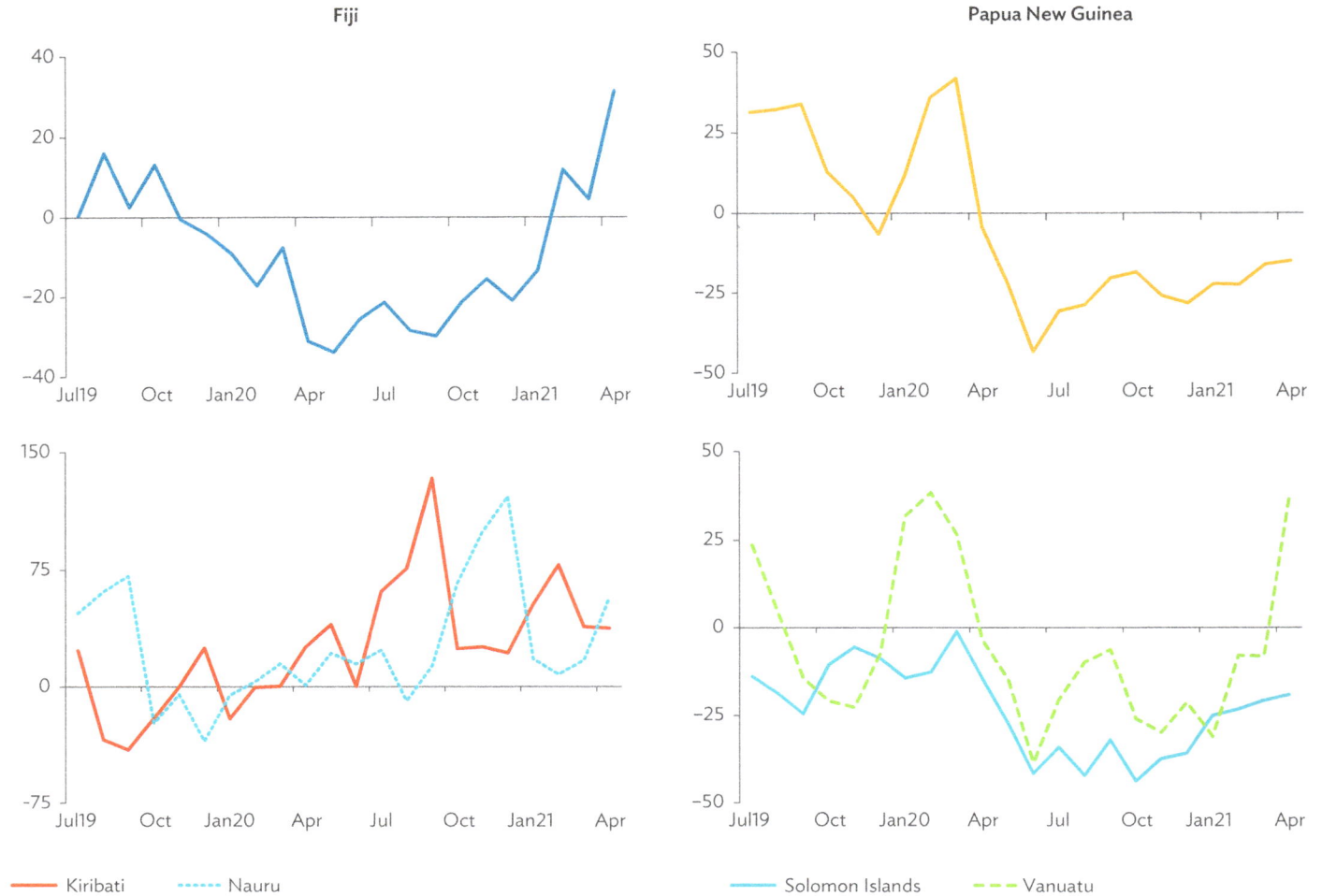

Fiji

Papua New Guinea

— Kiribati   ····· Nauru

— Solomon Islands   --- Vanuatu

A$ = Australian dollar, m.a. = moving average, rhs = right-hand scale, y-o-y = year-on-year.
Source: Australian Bureau of Statistics.

Nonfuel Merchandise Exports from New Zealand and the United States
(y-o-y % change, 3-month m.a.)

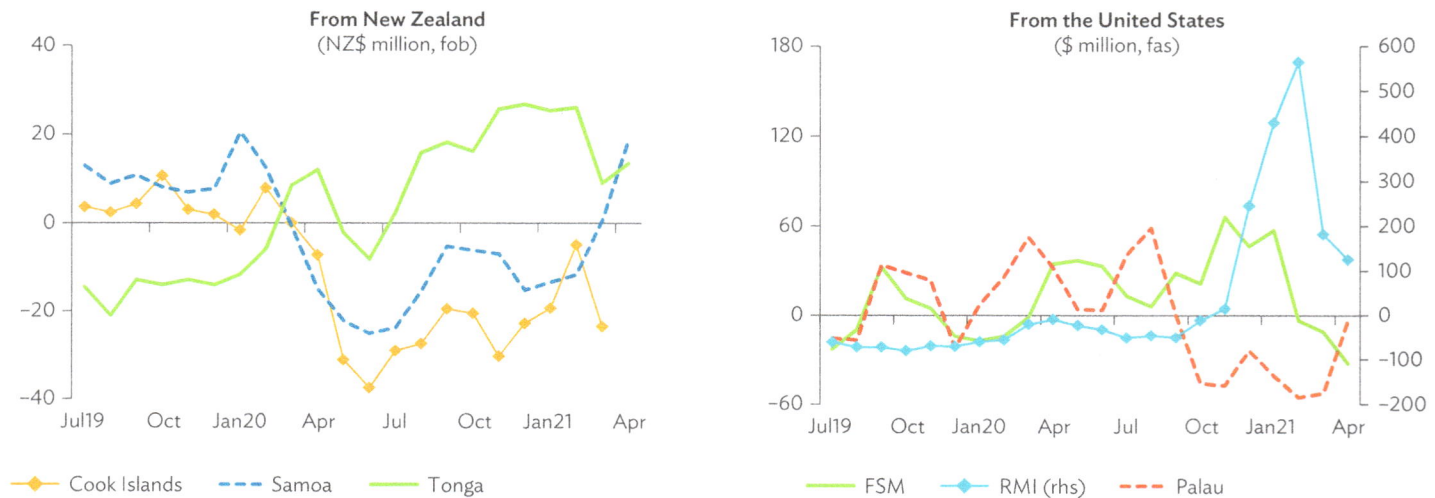

From New Zealand
(NZ$ million, fob)

From the United States
($ million, fas)

— Cook Islands   --- Samoa   — Tonga

— FSM   — RMI (rhs)   --- Palau

fas = free alongside, fob = free on board, FSM = Federated States of Micronesia, m.a. = moving average, NZ$ = New Zealand dollar, RMI = Republic of the Marshall Islands, y-o-y = year on year.
Sources: Statistics New Zealand and US Census Bureau.

Diesel Exports from Singapore
(y-o-y % change, 3-month m.a.)

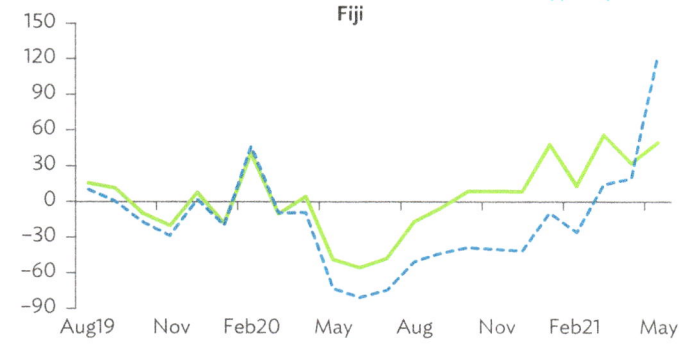

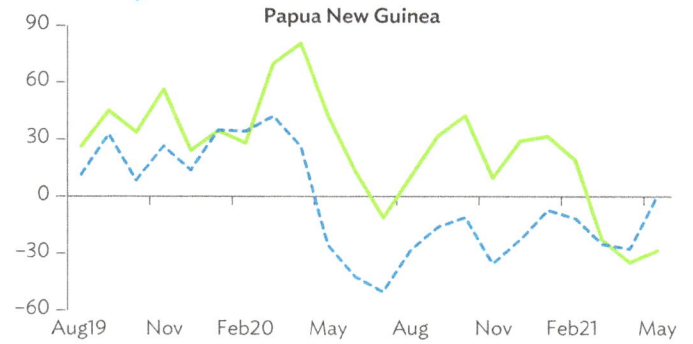

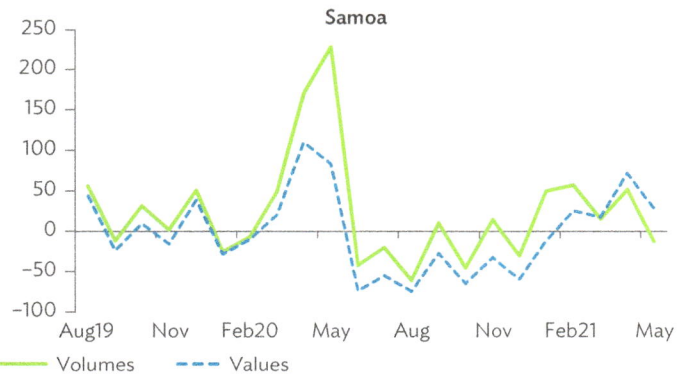

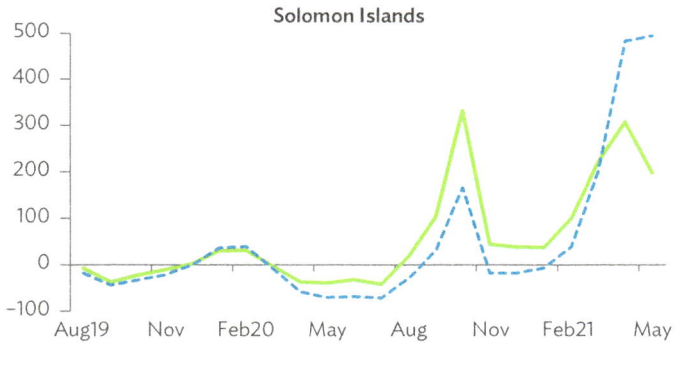

Fiji

Papua New Guinea

Samoa

Solomon Islands

Volumes — — — Values

m.a. = moving average, y-o-y = year on year.
Source: International Enterprise Singapore.

Gasoline Exports from Singapore
(y-o-y % change, 3-month m.a.)

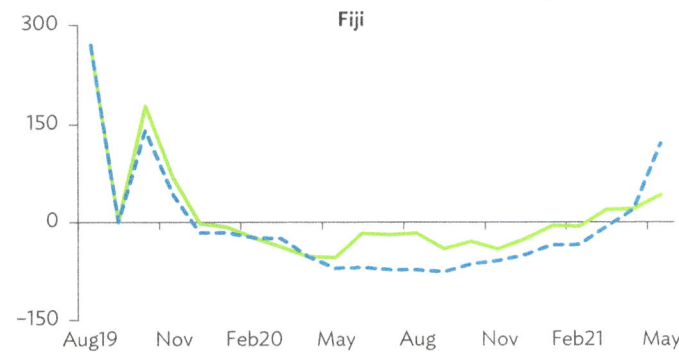

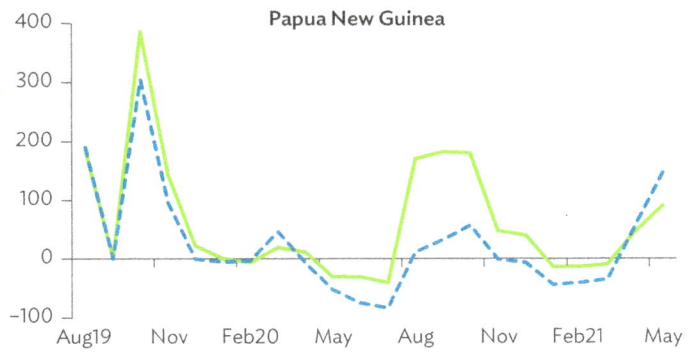

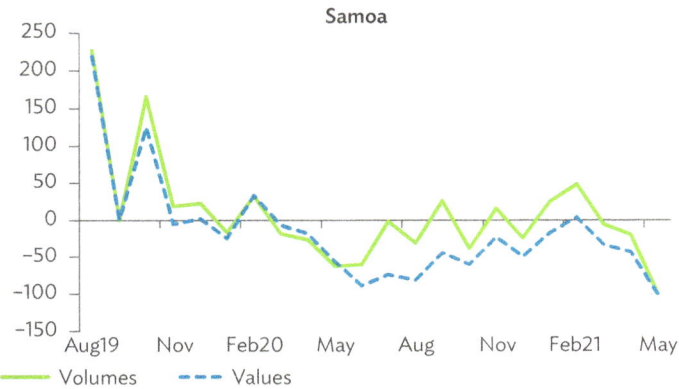

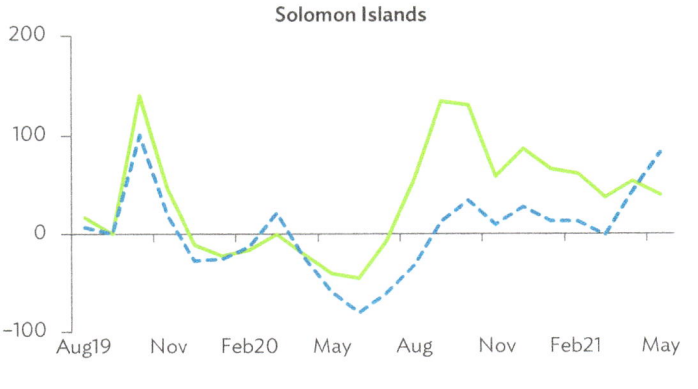

Fiji

Papua New Guinea

Samoa

Solomon Islands

Volumes — — — Values

m.a. = moving average, y-o-y = year on year.
Source: International Enterprise Singapore.

Departures from Australia to the Pacific
(monthly)

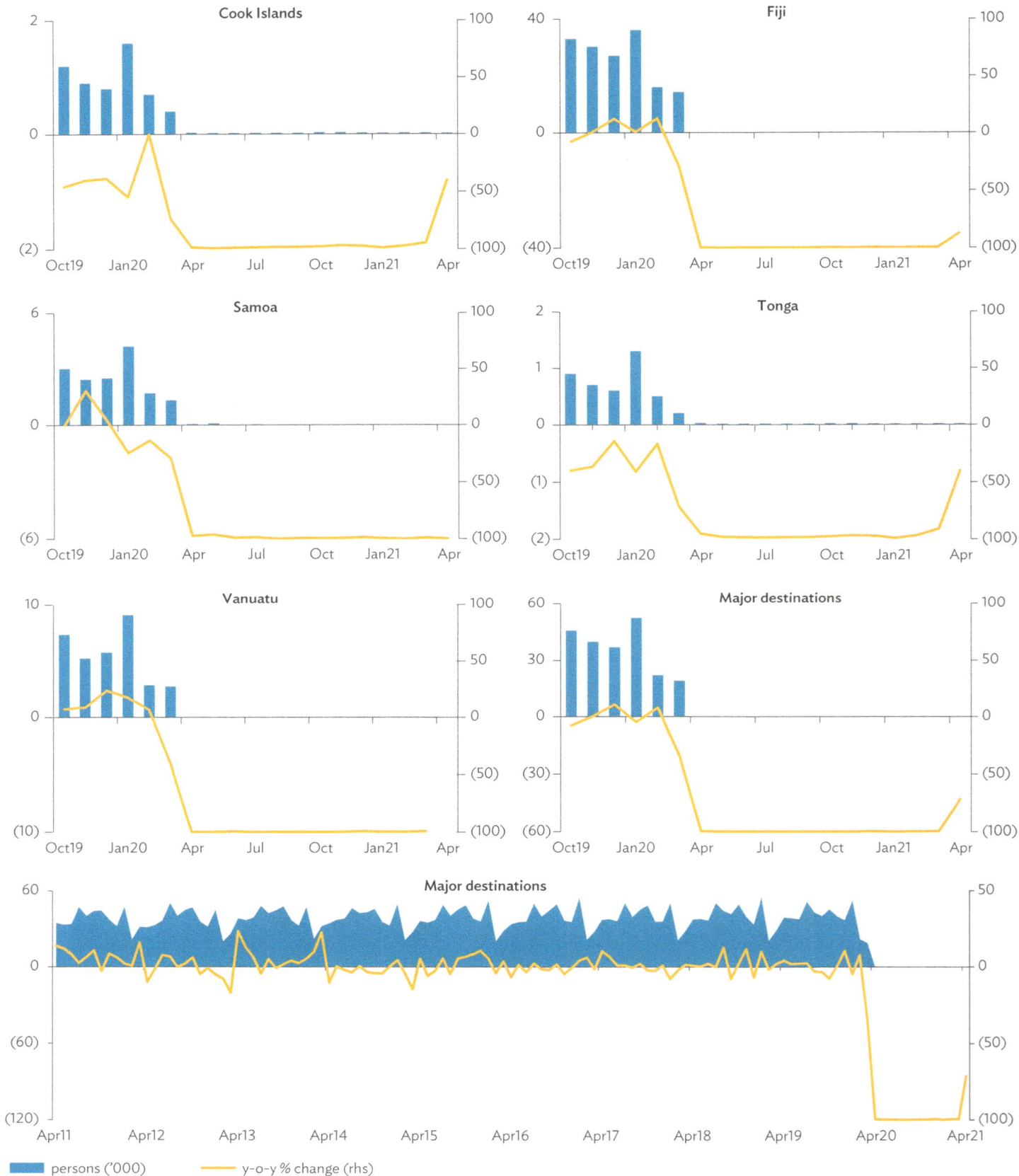

Cook Islands

Fiji

Samoa

Tonga

Vanuatu

Major destinations

Major destinations

persons ('000)   y-o-y % change (rhs)

rhs = right-hand scale, y-o-y = year on year.
Source: Australian Bureau of Statistics.